Vanessa's Top Ten T[...]
Navigating Your Un[...] journey

- Communicate with staff and each other.
- If you have questions—ask!
- Turn up, take part, do the work.
- Get organized and plan ahead with your assignments.
- Embrace technology, but stay safe online.
- Budget your finances carefully.
- Learn to balance the professional and personal sides of your life.
- Look after yourself and your mental health.
- Don't struggle or suffer in silence, always (always) ask for help.
- Enjoy your academic journey!

The Pocket Guide for Students

The Pocket Guide for Students

Navigating Your University Journey

By Vanessa Parson

OXFORD
UNIVERSITY PRESS

OXFORD
UNIVERSITY PRESS

Great Clarendon Street, Oxford, OX2 6DP,
United Kingdom

Oxford University Press is a department of the University of Oxford.
It furthers the University's objective of excellence in research, scholarship,
and education by publishing worldwide. Oxford is a registered trade mark of
Oxford University Press in the UK and in certain other countries

Published in the United States of America by Oxford University Press
198 Madison Avenue, New York, NY 10016, United States of America

British Library Cataloguing in Publication Data
Data available

Library of Congress Control Number: 2022948346

ISBN 978-0-19-886523-0

Printed in the UK by
Bell & Bain Ltd., Glasgow

This book is dedicated to you, the reader and future graduate.
I wish you the very best of luck on your university journey.

Brief Table of Contents

Detailed Contents

7. ACCESSING UNIVERSITY SUPPORT
   AND LOOKING AFTER YOUR MENTAL
   HEALTH 143

Acknowledgements

Thank you, first and foremost, to all my students, past and present; without you asking a mindboggling number of questions and allowing me access to the dreaded 'rumour mill', I would never have had the idea for this book in the first place. Thank you also for your kindness and generosity in sharing some fabulous, and occasionally hilarious, advice for future students. I had far more quotations than we were able to fit into the book and I hope future students find your words of wisdom helpful. You are all amazing individuals who work so unbelievably hard, despite a myriad of challenging circumstances; never forget how much you've accomplished, and I'm proud of you all.

Thanks also go to my colleagues, both past and present, and friends, for providing copious support for this project, some brilliant advice, suggestions, and for sharing cross-institutional differences with me so I could provide as broad a scope as possible to support students without causing unnecessary confusion. I really hope this book helps a little with some of the challenges we are all facing in the higher education sector at the moment.

I'd also like to thank my editors for their, frankly brilliant, edits and helpful advice throughout the process of writing this book: Martha Bailes, Nicola Hartley, and latterly Grace Howard. Your contributions, expertise, and support mean a huge amount, and this book would most certainly not be as clear and coherent as it is without you. Thank you to Martha and Nicola for your patience and detail-focused approach to edits. Grace, thank you for picking up this book in the final stages and ensuring it reaches its intended audience. Martha, thank you for understanding what I was trying to achieve in my early ideas, and for trusting me to bring this book to life; I will endeavour to complete all the sentences in a first draft next time!

Finally, and most importantly, I'd like to thank my daughter Libby, whose love, patience, and calm acceptance of the writing and academic sides of my life sometimes taking up a lot of time has helped give me the support and confidence to complete this book and achieve more than I thought possible. You are growing into an amazingly kind, considerate, and intelligent young woman, and I'm so proud of you.

Editorial Advisory Panel

Oxford University Press would like to thank the following individuals who gave their time to review draft material from the book. Your feedback was invaluable and is greatly appreciated.

Academic panel

Hannah Bannister, Imperial College London
Michael Berry, University of Sheffield
Lesley Black, University of Winchester
Kerry Blagden, University of Lincoln
Stuart Bullen, University of Brighton
Wendy Garnham, University of Sussex
Dr Stephanie McKendry, University of Strathclyde

Student panel

Daniel Debra Asare, University of Plymouth
Emma Berwick, University of Birmingham
Harvey Brehony, Keele University
Tiffany Burgess-Trott, Arden University
Ricardo Pereira Carvalho, London Metropolitan University
Kateryna Chuprina, Arden University
Roman Coussement, University of Manchester
Francesca Daw, Anglia Ruskin University
Bethany Dow, University of Dundee
Holly English, University College Dublin
Orlagh Fraser, University of Aberdeen
Dexin Gao, University College London
Rocio Garcia, London Metropolitan University
Salma Ghandour, University of Manchester
Risha Ghosh, SOAS University of London

Daniel Guerra, Aberystwyth University
Romilly Hryczanek, University of Reading
Joseph Ingle, University of Lincoln
Megan Irvine, University of Surrey
Joseph Jabra, Aston University
Martina Kalalova, Northumbria University
Rabinoor Khurana, University of Dundee
Kiran Kshatriya, University of Leicester
Chi Kuan Lei, Herriot-Watt University
Fraser Low, University of Dundee
Zoe Macpherson, University of Strathclyde
Maria Luisa Maroto, Oxford Brookes University
Dylan McAllister, University of Sunderland
Hal Meakin, University of Essex
Daniel O'Neill, Aberystwyth University
Casper Pachocki, Utrecht University, Netherlands
Mohamad Salam Perez, University of Southampton
Nicolas Persson, University of Dundee
Max Phippin, University of Warwick
Luke Pilkington, Queen Mary, University of London
Eva Pogacar, Herriot-Watt University
Antigoni Prevezanou, University of Piraeus, Greece
Dalia Puig, University of Dundee
Jacopo Razzauti, University of Dundee
Kathryn Revie, University of Dundee
Nora Vanessa Bonilla Rogel, London Metropolitan University
Salah Soomro, University College London
Edmund Strain, University of Warwick
Andrew Tinkler, University of Oxford
Paula Tomaszewska, University of Dundee
Priscilla Tomaz, Queen Mary, University of London
Rosie Underhill, University of Bath
Richard Vesely, University of Cambridge
Jonathan Winbow, University of Manchester

Preface

The idea for this book came about in 2019, when misunderstandings around how university worked and various rumour mill challenges caused considerable tension among students (and staff!). At the same time, despite the usual information provision for all undergraduates, colleagues across the country were seeing the same patterns indicating lack of understanding of how university works among the student population; unfortunately, this confusion has only increased since the COVID-19 pandemic began. As educators, we are aware that understanding is the first step on the road to performance; a lack of understanding can impact engagement, progression, retention—all things which make a big difference to success at university. The plan for this book was to tackle some of the misunderstandings *before* students get to university, give them advice and pre-university support they could take with them through their studies, which would make them would feel more confident and have a hugely beneficial impact on performance.

I wanted to create a 'how to' guide for university, answering those questions we get asked every year, explaining how university works, how to maximize success, and how to navigate the university experience. In other words, a 'pocket Vanessa', using all the knowledge I've learned over the years around how university works in the current educational climate, along with my knowledge about the psychology spheres of learning and university transition, all wrapped up in the personal tutoring style I've developed over the years.

Unfortunately I couldn't fit every single thing I wanted to share with you in my book, so it was really important to have an online component to accompany it, with extra resources and advice to support you in your journey through university. The Oxford Learning Link (www.oup.com/he/parson1e) will contain a time management guide, a financial planner and budgeting guide, a mindfulness and mental health guide, and all the tables and tips from the book.

I wanted this to be an interactive book which students could write in, refer to, and use as a basic manual for information and contacts if ever they needed support and help; for this reason there are lots of Tables and Boxes throughout for you to complete with information related to your university as needed, and I encourage you to write in them in the paperback version of this book. I also wanted a clear student voice; advice from peers can be far more powerful than an academic voice. There was an initial query as to whether I could get enough diverse student quotations to support this book, but I knew my wonderful students would come through for me; they provided some fantastic quotations (as did colleagues and friends) to support my advice. I'm fortunate that the team at Oxford University Press instantly saw the benefit in this style of book and have worked hard with me to make that a reality.

University is a profound transition point, not just in an educational sense. It is a period which marks the transition from known to unknown, before to after, less to more knowledge, and for many students it can mean a significant change in career prospects, regardless of the age they enter university. For international students, there is the transition to a new culture and educational system, alongside language challenges and moving away from home countries and support networks. For many students there are caring responsibilities and financial considerations. In addition, for students aged 18–25, this period of life marks the final big push of neural development where they are forming into their adult selves, developing independence, working out who they are, and what they want in life. It is only natural students find this period of life both challenging and intensely rewarding. With the increasing prominence of financial concerns and mental health needs, it is more important than ever that there is a clear understanding of how higher education works in order to minimize anxiety and ensure students know where to turn when they need support.

There is more government involvement in higher education nowadays, which has led to greater oversight of students within universities. We monitor attendance more closely and provide more support to students in all areas while they navigate their degrees and as they move into the workforce post graduation. In addition, we now have a greater awareness of the constantly changing student demographic, a better awareness of mental health needs, and a clear understanding of an evolving financial landscape which means student loans are a ubiquitous necessity.

We have a number of challenges ahead of us in higher education, some significant ones are around the impact of the pandemic on educational practice, retention, engagement, and academic integrity—all of which are covered here from a student perspective. I'm hoping this book reduces some of the natural anxiety around the transition to university, for both students and staff. But primarily, this book is designed to reduce student anxiety around the transition to university, and to ensure students know what awaits them through the oft-hallowed doors of universities—because forewarned is always forearmed.

My favourite quotation in the book is from Alice, my PhD student: 'Become the ringleader of your own circus.' It's great advice, but in order to do that, you first need to know how the circus works.

Vanessa

Chapter 1

INTRODUCTION

> Experience everything university throws at you ... there will be tears, tantrums, laughs, and smiles but most of all pride, for what you will achieve after it is all over.
>
> **Emma**

Congratulations, you've made the decision to go to university. The next few years are going to be filled with new experiences, plenty of surprises, lots (and lots) of new information, learning transferable skills, and, importantly, a Higher Education qualification—your degree. Welcome to the next phase of your learning experience!

I'm Vanessa, and I've written this book to help you through the transition to university, no matter what subject you're doing, what stage of life you are at, or which university you're going to. Going to university is a huge transition point in your life, but because it has become very much normalized to go to university (which can only be a good thing), the focus on this transition has been lost somewhat in many areas. This book is designed to help you tackle this transition to university; to help you understand how it all works, and to help support you throughout your first year of your degree, ensuring that you have the tools and skills to perform at your best in your academic work. Even with all the outreach programmes and Open Days universities have now, there are still some misconceptions floating around that cause anxiety to our students, and this book aims to resolve those as far as possible.

There has been a big change in recent years in how universities work, partly due to the impact of COVID-19 on the higher education sector. So there are a number of changes in how we teach you, how we're funded, and the types of students we now welcome through our doors. We're likely to see many more changes across the next few years, particularly now there is a move to incorporating more online elements to many courses following on from the COVID-19 pandemic. There are other 'survival guides' or 'success' books out there, but this one really is different. This book is the only one of its kind written by an academic, so you're getting the inside scoop on how university works now, what you can expect from us, and, crucially, what we expect from you.

I've watched as my students, many of whom have kindly contributed quotes for this book, have struggled and succeeded on their journey to getting their degrees. As academics we support all varieties of student, often through some extremely stressful and distressing situations. So, as universities and as academics, we have the resources in place to support our students with their individual needs and situations; all universities now have central support systems designed for this specific purpose. We know that everyone who comes through our doors is an individual who wants to achieve the best degree they can, but we're keenly aware of all the challenges many of you face during your lives. I've also seen many of the barriers which can impact this: finances, visas, mental health issues, stress, family issues, jobs, sickness, the list goes on. We know that life happens during the time you're with us, and helping you find the support you need is an important part of the transition phase, as well as throughout your time with us.

I've watched how our student population has changed beyond all recognition in recent years. Gone are the days when our students come predominantly from Sixth Form or college; now we have a rapidly expanding population from non-traditional routes, many of whom are juggling caring responsibilities and jobs alongside their studies. Universities are also now required to consider widening participation and equality and diversity requirements with the entire student body, so university is increasingly accessible for all. In addition, funding is completely different to when I went to university back in the 1990s; there are now various loans to negotiate, and lots (and lots) of forms to fill in; the vast majority of our student population work at least one job in addition to their academic studies so they can afford to come to university. Time and resources are much thinner on the ground than in previous years, and we are acutely aware of this.

> Don't be afraid to be open-minded. University is about experience and exploring curiosity. This is your opportunity to make a difference!
> **Hannah**

What I want to share with you is how university works, but also how you can help yourself succeed, despite any circumstances that you might find challenging during your studies. Many students think that because academics (your lecturers and tutors) are busy, we don't have time for them. This is absolutely not the case. Yes, we're busy, and most of us aren't counsellors, but supporting you is very much part of our role for the majority of academics in the UK. You will meet a wide variety of lecturers and support staff during your time at university, and I'm well aware that I'm at the friendlier end of the scale. But we will all know where you can get the help and support you are looking for, so if in doubt, please do talk to us. You should always let your tutor or lecturer know if there is something affecting you and your studies, and at every institution there are a wide range of policies, procedures, and support avenues in place just for supporting you throughout your degree.

But even though academics know how to access this information and support, it's even better if you do too as it gives you a sense of control over your time at university, and helps you feel just that bit more secure when you start with us. If you have already worked out where to get the support and information you need, then it saves you lots of emails and it means you get answers and support just a little bit quicker. A little bit of information about how University works will be incredibly helpful to you.

This text covers a huge range of material, from study skills to support and from fresher's week to finances. It is designed for you to dip in and out as needed, so there's no expectation you'll read chapters in order, and there's plenty of signposting throughout to encourage you to read the bits you need when you need to read them.

There are lots of quotations/messages from students throughout this book: they are from current students and former students, either that I know or that I teach/have taught. Some names are real, used with permission, some are pseudonyms. I hope their insight, experiences, and fantastic advice will help you on your journey through university.

I've been privileged to help a great many students over the years, and I love seeing them succeeding and graduating at the end of their degrees. With all the changes happening in universities, it's time to share that experience, and help you with your transition to what will hopefully be a rewarding and positive experience. University really can change your life for the better, and this book will help you transition to this next chapter in your lives, so you can really get the most out of your university experience. I wish you the very best of luck in the next phase of your studies, and I hope you enjoy your time at university.

> I wish I'd had this book to let me know what to expect.
>
> **Sarah**

Chapter 2

THE DIFFERENCE BETWEEN UNIVERSITY AND PRE-UNIVERSITY

Why This Chapter Is Important

- This chapter is all about how university is different from any previous education experience you've had so far, but it's also about giving you a better understanding of what's expected and how it all works.

> *Uni is a culture shock, but in the best way.*
>
> **Kallie**

There is a difference between where you've come from, educationally speaking, and where you're now heading, whatever path you have taken until now. For many students university life can be something of a culture shock, and occasionally it can seem a bit intimidating. Going to university for the first time can be a little bit like going on stage and performing a role in a play when everyone knows the lines except you, and it feels like they all expect you to instinctively know what to do next. We will give you the script outline for how it all works,

I promise, and this book will help you learn this script, but it is up to you to read the information we give you and fill in the details. The most important thing to remember is that if at any point you get stuck, you should ask for help.

I hope this chapter will help you understand the world you're about to enter a little better, and how doing a degree actually works (spoiler alert, we're *nothing* like your teachers or previous educators!).

Routes to University

> Everyone is on a different timeline; it doesn't mean your timeline's wrong.
>
> **Kallie**

Before we look in detail at what's expected at university, we need to first cover how you got here. There are many routes into university, and we have an increasing number of students who fall into the 'mature student' category (which means over the age of 21). There are multiple routes into university: the more 'traditional' routes of A levels, Scottish Highers, Irish Highers, and other college (level 3) qualifications. Alongside this there are qualifications such as Access or Foundations courses in England and Ireland, or SWAP (Scottish Wider Access Programme) or pre-entry courses in Scotland. I'll use the terms 'college access' or 'university access' course in this chapter to cover this variety of terms.

College access courses are delivered mainly through local colleges and cover a wide range of subjects relevant to your future degree, but also aim to 'bring you up to speed' in a number of core areas such as Maths, English, and Science. There tend to be broad categories of courses, and you are likely to do only do a small proportion of the topic you want to specialize in later on. You will still have to apply through UCAS to get a place at your university of your choice.

University access programmes are more specialized towards what you wish to study, and are now frequently run within universities but are sometimes run within local colleges with support from the universities. Typically, these courses will grant you automatic access to the first year of your chosen degree programme, so to change degree you may need to re-apply through UCAS (to your original or another university) or ask to transfer courses within the university you're registered at.

When you apply to university, you will find each course has a set number of 'points' which you achieve through Level 3 qualifications (equivalent to A Levels) approved by UCAS, although this does not include all Level 3 qualifications (e.g. some vocational courses and counselling courses). Sometimes students fall a little short of this number of points but have considerable prior learning or experience within the workplace that universities can take account of. This is particularly the case on university access degrees where we know we are teaching you the entry skills necessary for Level 4 (first year of your full degree programme).

This isn't the case for every programme—law and medicine are particularly difficult to get into and require top-level grades at most institutions. Plus, many subjects will have a set series of non-negotiable requirements due to professional body regulations. For example, Psychology students *must* have Level 2 (GCSE) Maths and English at the minimum pass grade (C/4 or equivalent) in order to get on to a professionally accredited degree and potentially do further study and/or training to work as a psychologist afterwards (a minimum of a lower-second honours degree is also required for further study and training).

Maths and English are the standard non-negotiable subjects at Level 2 (GCSE equivalent) so for everyone wanting to pursue a degree

I would advise making sure you have both. Many colleges run free Level 2 Maths and English courses if you're registered at the local university, so check these out and talk to your university—you may be able to complete these in tandem during your university access year. For anyone doing a college access course, it will likely be an automatic element on your course, and you will have access to these programmes within the college you're studying at.

So, if you don't quite meet the entry points for your chosen university access programme, make sure you apply anyway and include a lot of detail about your prior learning and experience. Within the university admissions systems there is often a method where we look at each application which doesn't meet the entry requirement and can decide on a case-by-case basis. Make sure you cover the functional skills aspects of your prior learning and work experience—don't skimp on detail in your personal statement, you never know, this may just help you get a place on your chosen course.

Finally, we have what's known as Clearing. This is where available places at universities are opened up to those who didn't quite make the original entry points target during August so that they can apply to get on to degree programmes. Lots of students don't get the grades they hoped for (I certainly didn't) and it's important to remember your grades don't define who you are, they are merely a stepping stone to what comes next. If you didn't get the grades you wanted in your pre-university exams, then you can go into Clearing via the UCAS website where all course vacancies are advertised and you can apply direct or arrange to speak to advisers who are on hand in every university, waiting to speak to prospective students. Clearing can be very stressful for students, not least as it's right off the back of disappointment they didn't get the grades they wanted or their first choice of university place. Clearing is an opportunity to broaden your horizons, so if you end up in this position, try not to worry, there are lots of courses available and you should have faith in yourself.

How Life at University Is Different

> Don't give up, it can seem daunting. Especially for mature students that have not done anything academic in years. It gets easier.
>
> **Deb**

Adjusting to university life can take time, especially if you have been used to very formalized learning beforehand, or if you have been out of education for a while. We find new students often need far more direction than we might expect, and while we are happy to provide this, we do expect students to take ownership of their learning during the first year of their studies. One of the biggest differences in university-level education is that you are expected to be an effective *independent* learner.

Your degree is just yours, and nobody else can do it for you. Lecturers are not the same as teachers, and we are also not the same as employers. We are learning facilitators, which means that you hold one of the keys to the learning experience—your engagement is a crucial part of the process, so we want you to engage in all the content we deliver and direct you to.

Lecturers and Teachers Are Very Different Animals

> You can have a laugh with your lecturers ... [but] even if you're friendly, remember respect ... be professional.
>
> **Sarah**

Before university, tutors, or teachers, work on a slightly more formal footing than most university lecturers these days. You possibly called teachers 'Miss' or 'Sir', while sometimes saying their full name, for example, Mrs Lumley. However, at university, just because we have titles like Dr or Professor, we're often known by our first names—please do call me Vanessa, because Dr Parson is *way* too formal. Some academics might prefer to be a bit more formal though, and in some institutions, it is standard practice to call academics by their formal titles. But most of the time, your lecturers will let you know what they wish to be called. As a general rule, follow what we write on our lecture slides, how we sign off our emails, and what you hear other students calling us. If you're not sure, just ask!

Another difference between lecturers and teachers is that lecturers teach lots of year groups and many modules, so we might not remember who you are for a little while. I'm great with faces and names but combining the two takes me a little while. It is much easier to remember students who interact with us a lot though, so chat to your lecturers if you can; talk to us in class, or make a point of emailing us if you have questions and prefer not to talk in class (don't forget to add your name to emails), and we'll find it much easier to pull your name out of the many we're trying to cram into our head each year. But please don't take it personally if your lecturer doesn't instantly learn your name. We have hundreds of students' names to learn each year, so be patient with us.

Unlike most teaching staff pre-university, most of your lecturers (or professors) are likely to have significant commitments outside of the lecture hall. Many are active researchers and/or professional practitioners alongside their teaching commitments. We're all actually called Academics, we are mostly trained as researchers initially and then we carry this on alongside teaching. What this means is that you're getting really up-to-date information in classes, particularly if we're teaching our specialist subjects. We will all have our own different styles and approaches to teaching, so you will likely get plenty of variety in who and how you are taught. You might get taught brand new information that hasn't even gone to press yet!

Differences between University-level Study and A level/College

> Look at your lecturers as a team and not teachers. They help you and you help them. They were once in the same position you were, don't be afraid to ask.
>
> **Shawnee**

As we've noted, university is a fair bit different from schools and colleges. I've taught A level (in a school and several colleges), and I've also taught at degree level across multiple institutions, and there is one very big difference between all these institutions—levels of formality. At university it is much more relaxed and informal than any school or college; even if you're at a college where you're on first name terms with the teachers, you're still expected to be in class on time every time, in suitable clothes and with the appropriate materials to learn with.

At university, we start from the basic principle that you're all adults and can look after yourselves for the most part. Support is available if you need it, but in class, we're going to get on with teaching. You will be expected to actively engage with, prepare for, and attend your lectures, tutorials, seminars, and/or labs (as applicable).

However, there are some elements of formality attached to your tuition in university. Sometimes you will get an email warning you about attendance or to ask why you've not submitted an assignment and if you're OK, but mostly we're going to assume you're fine unless we hear otherwise.

The only person responsible for passing your assignments and modules, and therefore getting a degree, is you. If you accidentally fall asleep in lectures (it does happen on occasion), make sure you read up on the material later on. We are expecting you to remember what we've talked about in lectures, so if you weren't paying quite as much

11

attention as you intended then you will need to ensure you do the work later to catch up. There is a lot of content to cover, and we do expect you to keep up.

Yes, we want you to engage and work hard, we really do, and we always want you to pay attention and learn. Ideally, you will attend and pay attention throughout every single one of your classes, because that's what you're paying to do—to learn. We do get that life can sometimes be distracting though, so if you have a bad day and don't really listen, just catch up later and show up ready to learn for the next class. If you need longer because life is throwing you curve balls, talk to your tutors to get support (see also Chapter 8). There is plenty of advice in this book for those times when life prevents you from keeping up (see Chapters 6, 8, and 13), but for the most part if you prioritize partying over studying then you only have yourselves to complain to if you're behind.

But for most courses, we genuinely don't care if your hair is rainbow coloured and are unlikely to comment if you're a bit scruffy, because it doesn't matter for learning. In fact, you'll find that many staff also take a more relaxed approach to their appearance. Some may have tattoos and piercings, while others dress casually; I normally wear jeans to work. Nothing about your appearance changes what is between your ears (your brain) and that's the bit we're interested in developing. Turn up, listen, engage, and learn, that's what we want. Welcome to freedom from school/college appearance restrictions.

Of course, there are some courses where appearance is something to be aware of. Certain courses, such as Nursing, Law, or Occupational Health, will require you to wear a uniform of sorts, at least in some areas of the course. For any course where a placement is an integral part, please ensure that you have the required clothing ready, clean, and ironed for those days you need it. Being presentable is an important feature in many areas of employment, and this is something that some courses expect right from the start of your studies. You may also find that there are regulations around piercings and hair colour as well. Be aware of the regulations around what you can and can't wear, so that you're able to negotiate those effectively during your studies.

Differences between University-level Study and Other Education Routes (Access Courses)

Since starting university . . . I feel as though anything is possible now as my horizon has widened which has made me look at things differently and filled me full of confidence.

Jamie

There are fewer differences between university study and other educational routes, particularly if you did a university access year in the university you wish to study in. You will have a headstart in terms of learning to manage your time and complete work in the way we expect at university, because your course is often taught in, or in conjunction with, a university.

However, students who undertake other education routes, such as college access courses, are typically mature students (over the age of 21). As a mature student, you will have to integrate your course into your current life, and that's the biggest challenge for students coming from other educational backgrounds than A level or college, as you may well have to juggle your existing job and family commitments. Planning, scheduling, getting a wall calendar, they all help. If you plan your time, things will go a lot more smoothly.

What you are likely to notice during your degree is less handholding compared to a college or university access course. As with those coming straight from A levels, you will notice that classes may not be as structured as they were previously. The section on independent learning later in this chapter is a must-read, although you will have had slightly more practice than those who have come straight from A level, both from your college or university access year and from your previous work experiences. Make the most of this headstart.

Getting to Classes

> *Speak to your lecturers they are friendly people, and human too!*
> **Alice**

Commuting to class is increasingly becoming a normal part of university life, with many students now choosing to live at home or some distance from university. It has therefore become a significant factor to think about while at university. Gone are the days when the majority of students fell out of bed and into lectures after a short walk. Commuting is often now a central part of the study day, and can sometimes be a challenge, particularly if you need to do the school run first or there are transport issues such as roadworks, or train delays. Take a look at BOX 2.1 for tips on planning your travel.

It's important to remember that you need to stay safe on your commute to and from university. Make sure you have a copy of the local transport network timetable on your phone, so that you are able to plan your route safely and effectively, as far as possible. If walking, pay attention to which routes are busy, well-lit, and include main roads, and are therefore likely to be a bit safer, particularly at night. Make sure you're aware of which routes are more likely to be unsafe, particularly at night. For example, routes that include an underpass or unlit, quiet streets might not be safe at night, so you might want to avoid those. Similarly, walking through the park during the day may be fine, but at night it might be poorly lit. Transport links are often not as reliable as the timetables would have us believe, so always have a back-up commuting plan if you can; make sure local taxi numbers or apps are stored on your phone. If cycling, it could be a good idea to do a 'test run' of a chosen route outside of 'rush hour' so you can get a feel for the route (and adjust if needed) while traffic is slightly quieter.

Commuting comes with the knowledge that there will be occasional transport issues (e.g. snow, crashes, delays on public transport, parking challenges). While you do need to plan your time appropriately and negotiate your lives so you get to class on time, we know there will be the odd occasion you cannot avoid, which will delay you getting to class. If this occurs, just let your module leader know (see BOX 2.3 for a place to write the names of your module leaders and their email/contact details).

BOX 2.1 Planning Your Travel

It might sound fairly obvious, but you will need to check you have access to relevant travel information you need to get to class. Here's a list of things you need to check before you start classes—tick when you have sorted out all that apply to you.	
If you're walking:	
I know the safest route to take to/from university during the day	
I know the safest route to take to/from university at night, or the method of transportation I need to use to get safely home	
If you're cycling:	
I know the safest route to take (which may/may not include cycle lanes, or permitted cycle paths through parks, etc.)	
I have working lights, both front and back (when it's dark, this is a legal requirement in the UK)	
I have a bike lock/chain, and I know where the bike racks are	

(Continued)

15

BOX 2.1 Continued

If you're taking public transport:	
I have a Metro/Underground/Bus/Tram timetable	
I know how much my mode of public transport costs (and have set aside the money to pay for it)	
I have bought/got a travel pass (you may get this free or discounted through your university)	
I know how long it takes to get to/from uni in the morning	
I know how long it takes to get to/from uni in the afternoon	
I know how long it takes to get to/from uni in the evening	
If you're driving:	
I have access to an app to aid navigation and show traffic levels (such as Google Maps or Waze)	
I know where the best parking options are	
I know how much parking costs (and have enough change ready/downloaded the payment app)	

We're fully aware of these challenges (often facing them ourselves), so we understand. Most universities are working on the challenges for students getting to class, and while we can't promise lectures and classes at 'easy' times of the day, you should get advance warning of when classes are (your timetable is often available when you register at the start of each academic year) and we will give you as much notice as we can for any class changes.

While we always prefer it if you attend on time, if you turn up a few minutes late with your pyjamas still on, very few of us mind on those courses where we don't have a dress code. We might glare at you if you're really late but as long as you're quiet (and don't interrupt if someone is talking) when you sit down, it's fine. If it's a small-group class, remember that a quick apology goes a long way. Just get on with engaging with the remainder of the class as best you can and catch up with what you missed later in your own time.

What you do have to remember about turning up to lectures late is that you have a right of entry so you should be allowed into the class. Some lecturers might not like students turning up late, but it's important to remember you cannot be excluded from class if you are late. Make sure you check your own university policy on lecture entry—available through the student manual/policy that should be easily available via your university website. Note down where your university's policies are located in BOX 2.2.

We do, however, appreciate a heads-up (as long as it's safe to do so) if you're going to be missing class. If you or your child is sick, or you're stuck for transport and, short of sprouting wings and flying, you're not able to get to class, then just let us know. BOX 2.3 is a handy resource to make sure you know who to contact for each of your modules.

It's worth remembering that we *do* know when all the student nights are in the local pubs and clubs! Not all lecturers will agree with me here, but I've always much preferred students drag themselves into class after a student night, complete with hangover cure (as long as it's not too smelly). I'd rather you heard five minutes of my class than none at all (although I'd rather you didn't do this every week!). On occasion, this is fine.

BOX 2.2 Student Learning Policy

Student Learning/Policy Details	Location Online

BOX 2.3 Who to Contact on Each Module When You Will Be Unavoidably Delayed or Absent from Class

Module	Name of Lecturer/Tutor for that Class	Their Email Address

Who's in Charge of My Course?

> People shouldn't be afraid to ask the lecturers questions.
>
> **Milo**

Ultimately the university and the Heads of School/Department oversee your degree, but all programmes have something called a Programme Leader (sometimes known as a Programme Manager or Course Leader, precise terms may vary) who is the person who runs your course on a day-to-day basis and has operational control over what happens. Your Programme Leader is the person responsible for your programme and everything connected to it from an academic perspective. If you get stuck or have any major problems (of any kind), then they are your first port of call.

BOX 2.4 **Programme Leader/Director Contact Details**

| Programme Leader/Manager: |
| Email address: |
| Availability day and time: |
| Where I can find them: |

Find out what their email address is, and find out when they are available so you can drop in (something we often call 'Office Hours' or 'Availability Hours', although different universities may have different labels for this). Write this information in BOX 2.4 so it's easy to find later on when you need it.

Learning Differences

> University is so different in the sense that you are given that freedom and are treated like an adult, but still have the support there if you need it.
>
> **Beth**

One of the biggest differences is that at university we are not going to be holding your hand through assignments and classes. At school/college there are worksheets, a curriculum, and a set series of tasks for you to complete, all of which feed into an assignment or exam, and you are going to be helped at most stages. At university we are guiding you to learn, not always specifically telling you what precise things to learn. When it comes to the theory elements of your course, we will show you the roadmap and then leave you to it; after we've gone through the basics, we expect you to do the rest. Just make sure you ask if you have questions.

The section on independent learning covers this in more detail. However, any practical elements of your course will have considerably more direction and support. It is worth remembering that some subjects, particularly STEM subjects (Science, Technology, Engineering, and Maths) have a lot of contact time simply because there are many more practical elements to these courses.

Motivate Yourself!

> Independent learning is huge, you have to start taking responsibility for your own learning.
>
> **Alex**

At school or college, you will have had a group of teachers whom you saw every week, you were expected to be in class, and the adults who looked after you were phoned if you skipped class. If you have a job and you don't show up, you get a phone call and potentially lose money if you skip a shift. At university, while we sometimes chase you if you don't attend much, you are expected to motivate yourselves to get to class and complete the work we set. That, in itself, is one of the biggest things you're going to need to do at university.

You're coming to university to get a degree, that's amazing, and we're thrilled you're on your way (we really are, we always look forward to meeting our new students). But you're coming to university old enough to vote and get married; we will support you in your development, but you're still an adult who can make your own decisions. Freedom is yours, use it wisely.

It is, however, completely normal to not love all elements of your course, or to find some elements more difficult than others. Your subject of choice contains a large number of things that you might not be aware of prior to beginning your degree, or if you were aware you may have underestimated their importance. For example, in Psychology, students often underestimate the importance of statistics and the, sometimes surprising, variety of subjects that actually come under the umbrella term of 'Psychology'. This can lead to frustration and occasionally a drop-off in motivation when the subject matter becomes more difficult. What is important to remember is that everything your lecturers are teaching you has a point and purpose in the grand scheme of your subject and your degree. Not all of it will be absolutely what you love, and not all of it will be easy. But you're doing a degree; this isn't reality TV or the movies, you're here to learn and that requires effort and motivation, both of which are entirely under your control.

If you don't do the reading for a seminar, you get to sit in the seminar watching everyone else learn and wondering what is going on, and you will not get the benefit we intended when we set the work. If you don't read your feedback from an assignment then make the same mistakes in the next one, and you won't improve. If you don't understand the feedback from assignments, ask for clarification from your lecturers.

Often students 'swipe' into classes now, using their student cards to do so. You may have to record your attendance in this way now, so this means not forgetting your student card! If you forget your card or you forget to swipe in, then you may need to let the system know (sometimes through an app or the website, check the procedure at your university) or you risk getting an email about attendance. If you've lost your card, you will need to replace your card (this may cost money, so keep it safe). If you're someone who loses their cards regularly, get a lanyard or put your card somewhere you can't forget it (such as in the car, your purse/wallet/attach it to your keys). Student cards typically now contain digital information that gives you access to the library, halls of residence, classes, and all sorts of things. They are your one-stop pass to all things at university, so you need to keep them safe.

In and after classes, we won't always check if you did the work we set, we just expect you to do it. The exception here, for most universities, is submitting formal assignments. Due to external pressures, some universities have started to follow up with students who don't submit their assignments, mostly to check everything is OK and to check if you need any support. If you don't submit an assignment, it's helpful to beat your lecturer to that email and contact us first. We'll cover what to do in the case of non-submissions in Chapter 4.

───────── **VANESSA'S TOP TIPS** ─────────

for motivation

> Plan and prioritise, don't leave things to the last minute.
>
> **Louis**

- Start (and maintain) a daily routine
  - If you regularly do something at a particular time (e.g. brush your teeth) then it becomes automatic to do this every day. Take that attitude into planning your study; if you develop a routine that works for you then you're more likely to maintain that through periods where your motivation dips.

- Break things down and plan your time
  - Big tasks like assignments can feel overwhelming, and this can lead to procrastination and delays in starting. Break down the things you need to do on each module into smaller and more easily accessible tasks. Organize them and do them one at a time. You'll find that it's much easier, and less overwhelming, to complete big pieces of work if you've done the earlier tasks (like reading and class activities) first.

- Don't expect to understand everything straight away
  - Accept that some things will be a challenge and you will need to do work to develop understanding. Once you accept that sometimes things will be difficult, it's a lot easier to keep going when something isn't easy straight away.

- Track your progress
  - You won't work at a consistent pace every day, so keep track of your progress so you can see how far you've come. It's amazing what 'little and often' can achieve.
- Allow for variety in your daily routine
  - We can't do the same thing all the time, it gets really dull. Break up your time and include things you enjoy, but make sure you vary what you do so that you're always interested.
- Form a study group
  - A supportive network of friends and study buddies can help keep you motivated on days when you've got a bit less 'get up and go'.

We are more than happy to support you if you contact us. If you have questions, email us; if you are struggling, email or talk to us; if you feel like you're stuck in quicksand or treading water/slowly sinking amid all this new information, definitely come and see us. But we can't help if we don't know what is going on, so if you're unsure, talk to us. But don't turn off the motivation and enthusiasm for your studies when things get tough, getting a degree is a big deal, and you'll need to work hard, but you don't have to do that without support.

Independent Learning Is a Thing—Roll with It

> *Motivation and independent learning—not gonna lie, it is hard. Take your time and break it down. Don't panic about the whole course or module, do one thing at a time.*
>
> **Kathy**

One of the biggest things you will need to master at university is independent learning: this is the reason you'll need lots of motivation. Some of you are going to love this aspect of higher education, and for some of you it means unlearning quite a lot of habits you've learned during your pre-university years. One of those habits could be related to the 'do this then do that and now you're done' approach—something that rarely happens in higher education.

While you're at school or college (either recently or in the past) there is typically a lot of direction given to you, lots of instructions, weekly homework (that you all did, right?), and a teacher guiding you through the syllabus. Then you get to university, and we give you some lectures, seminar work, discussion threads, a reading list, and a couple of assignment titles and expect you to just get on with it. OK, we're not quite that brutal, we give you plenty of support during your first year, and we do understand you've come from a different style of learning. But even so, for most of you this may still be something of a culture shock and can be incredibly daunting; coming from a place of intense structure to a place with a noticeable lack of it can be disorienting and take a while to get used to. Even with online, distance, and hybrid learning (more on those later), you will still find that there is less direction than pre-university styles of teaching.

Unlike in school or college, we cannot teach you everything in class: these are big topics we're dealing with now, including cutting-edge research and really up-to-date information, and there is a huge amount to cover. We can't do it in the few hours we see you each week; there's only so much we can cover in a lecture, so we need you to read and engage with the rest. As I mentioned above, we give you the roadmap but we expect you to follow it.

Each module you get will have contact hours attached to it, these are lectures and seminars/workshops/laboratory/practical classes. Your reading lists get you started on your module journey and are often available before your course starts. For your classes, we give you handouts to guide your learning (typically digitally, and in advance where this is possible, in line with legal requirements), and we give you lots of information in lectures, and (via your digital course pages) to scaffold your reading. We do expect you to expand on that with what we directly ask you to read though; go looking for lots of books and articles that are connected with the subject we're teaching you. If you find something interesting, let us know! I genuinely love it when students send me articles and books they've found and think I'll like; it expands my reading as well as their own, and they get to contribute to the following year's reading list and improve the module. But, ultimately, you are going to need to read a lot while you're at university. Fun fact, it's actually called 'reading for a degree', there's a hint in there somewhere.

Sometimes there are additional challenges around reading and independent learning at university. For those of you who have any additional learning difficulties, such as dyslexia, the reading list and independent learning expectations can be somewhat daunting. While you may need to develop new strategies for how to read what you need to, you might also need to get some support with this. Remember that we have teams of staff to help you do just that, sometimes within the library, sometimes within support services (there are various names for these, but all universities have a central team dedicated to student support). Remember, take things at your own pace when it comes to reading, use the strategies that help you, but don't ignore the fact the reading and independent learning have to be done. If you need some help, remember to ask for it.

Our goal is not to throw you in at the deep end, we will help you learn independently. To enable you to read through the bits we can't cover directly, we will give you reading lists and additional materials. We structure things a bit more in the first year, then taper this off as you go through your degree. Once you leave university you should have the skills to learn any topic completely by yourself, without anyone giving you assignments to motivate you. So, don't just rely on the material you're given in class, embrace the reading list and go for it.

You will need to know where to get the reading lists for your modules. Often there are links within the modules, and we will specify a core text that you need to focus on, something that we know will cover what you need for that module. In BOX 2.5 you can list the core texts and where to find your reading lists for each module during your first year.

However, if you're not fan of reading for fun, I'd suggest starting now. Reading supports your writing development and increases understanding of your subject. You don't want to fall into the academic misconduct trap simply due to making mistakes through lack of understanding (see Chapter 6), so make sure you do plenty of reading.

While we want you to use academic reading material in your work, we want you to read widely around this academic material as well. We really don't care what you read, just read, a lot. Read novels, newspapers, magazines, non-fiction books, blogs—it's all reading and it's all going to help with your learning (and your writing,

BOX 2.5 Finding Reading Lists and Core Texts

Module	Core Text(s)	Reading List Location

something you will need to do regardless of subject). If you're not sure what kind of books you like reading, go to your local library and get a bunch out to try, or spend an afternoon there and talk to the librarian for ideas. Accessing lots of different writing styles is beneficial for developing your writing style and ability, so try to read throughout your degree.

If you want to do well at university, my biggest piece of advice is that the more you read the better you'll do. Read at your own pace, using the strategies that work for you, but make sure you read. Every little bit you read will improve your knowledge, your understanding, and your writing. Once you're in the habit of reading more, university, and writing assignments, is going to get a whole lot easier.

Life Online: Virtual Learning Environments

> [The VLE] is useful and is really user friendly. Everything you could possibly ever need is right at your fingertips.
>
> **Dylan**

One big difference between schools, colleges, and universities is the type of digital support you get. Some of you will have used a Virtual Learning Environment (VLE), either through a school system or at college. VLEs are a digital teaching platform, and we use them to support learning and deliver materials. Some of you will also have had a very structured digital learning environment where tasks are allocated and marked, some of you may have had a VLE that you barely used.

In university we all now use this thing called a VLE, and it will become central to your learning, whatever type of degree you do. We've had VLEs for several decades, but they have become absolutely central

BOX 2.6 Where You Can Get Technical Support

Department technician name/email	
Online IT resource location	
VLE: 'How to' guide location	

to educational delivery since the COVID-19 pandemic. There are a few common VLEs in university (Canvas and Blackboard are particularly common) but sometimes universities develop their own systems in-house. They all have the same function though—centralized digital provision of your course materials and information. Many of you, in particular mature students, will not have used anything like it before. Don't worry, there's always a 'How To' guide available.

What you need to remember is that you do need to learn to use the VLE; you can't get through university without knowing how to access it and submit your work. Everything you need will be on your VLE so make sure you check your module pages for information regularly, and remember that we've probably anticipated a lot of your questions, so check the student and module guides we put up before you send us emails to ask. My advice is to become very familiar with the VLE as quickly as you can once you start university. If you get stuck, just ask the technical team for help (see BOX 2.6).

A Final Word

> *Always aim higher than you think you can achieve!*
>
> **Faye**

University is very different to most other learning formats, but that is what makes it such an exciting and rewarding experience. *You* will be in charge of your own learning, and *you* get to find out all the things you ever wanted to about your subject under the expert guidance of your lecturers. University is a really big step into a better future.

www.oup.com/he/parson1e

Visit the online resources where you will find additional materials including guides on time management, financial planning and budgeting, mindfulness and mental health, hints and tips, as well as all the tables from the book.

Chapter 3

FINANCE

Why This Chapter Is Important

- Money is a crucial consideration at university, with fees and loans now something you need to think about, along with rent and paying bills. Finance is a key area of your university journey where you get a lot of information very quickly. This chapter breaks down this information for you so that you're aware of the information that will help with your own financial situation.

- The UK is an educational destination for international and European students, and the financial considerations are slightly different for those students. This chapter covers the information you need and directs you to additional sources of information that are regularly updated.

> *To try and stay on top of my finances, I opened a[n online/*
> *app-based] account and had all earned wages paid into there to*
> *use as a social spending money, and kept my maintenance loan*
> *in my regular bank account to use for all my outgoings. I've found*
> *it's been a great way of knowing how much money you have for*
> *socializing and also a good way of saving as you usually have some*
> *left over by the time the next loan comes about!*
>
> **Shane**

It's really important to think about finances before starting your university course. Knowing how you are going to fund your studies and yourself during your studies is a significant factor that can, in part, determine whether you succeed or not at university.

Your main source of financial guidance at university will be a dedicated Student Finance Team, which most universities have in place, sometimes with a dedicated international team for overseas students. They can help you navigate the different processes and explain things that you might find a little confusing. In addition, they can direct you to additional sources of funding outside the student loan systems in the place where you study. Before you start university, or soon after you get there, check out the university website for more details. The Student Finance Teams will have their own page with a wealth of information available to support you, and all the contact details you need.

All university courses in the UK have a fee associated with them, which is split into two categories: HOME and OVERSEAS. Students from the UK are subject to the Home fees, and EU and International students are subject to the Overseas fees. Most UK students will get access to multiple student loans, and learning the difference between these, and how they work, will be vital for ensuring financial security while you're at university. However, there are also sources of financial support and incentives for EU and International-al students.

This chapter will also cover what the many sources of advice available online *don't* tell you; the financial consequences for non-attendance and withdrawal from the programme. In the second part of this chapter, we will look at budgeting, managing your income from all sources, including any paid work you do, and provide advice if you are new to managing money and/or could do with some support in this area.

University Student Finance Teams

> *Don't ask an academic . . . go to someone who knows: e.g. from a student advice centre or similar.*
>
> **Liz**

Every university has a dedicated team of staff to support students with their finances and provide financial advice. The student finance team can liaise with the official Student Loan team for you, support you in your applications for student finance, and give you advice when you're in financial difficulties. In BOX 3.1 you'll find a list of teams and roles

BOX 3.1 Your University Financial Support Team

Person/Service	Contact Information/Email
Student Finance Team	
Student Advice Team (sometimes called Well-being)	
Personal Tutor	
Chaplain/Religious Leader	
Another Lecturer I know/trust	

you might find at your university, make sure you fill in the contact details and names (if applicable) of key individuals who might be in a position to help you if you need it in the future.

What Is Student Finance?

> Have a second bank account, either a savings account or just a second account, and have your student loan go into that account. This removes temptation to spend it all at once and stops you thinking you have money waiting to be spent. Instead transfer yourself a weekly or monthly budget, it makes it a lot easier to stick your budget. Once you have come to the end of the month or week, if you have money left over treat yourself or save it!
>
> **Nicole**

Student finance is the term used for the money that is available to you in the form of loans, bursaries, and grants while you are a student at university. The student financial loans are the most common element of this, and almost all undergraduates take out student financial loans during their studies. The vast majority of Higher Education institutions are aligned with government regulations for universities and have degree-awarding powers, so you are eligible for student loans. If your university is not aligned with government regulations (e.g. if your degree is awarded by a different institution rather than the one you will attend) then you will not be eligible for student loans and you should talk to the Student Finance Team where you are going to university about your options for finance during your course.

The Different Types of Loans

There are two key types of student financial loan available to you at the majority of universities in the UK nations (with some variations in how they work and are applied): the student fees loan, and the student maintenance loan.

- The student fees loan is the money you may receive for covering the cost of your university tuition. This is money you will effectively never see; it gets handed directly to the university.

- The student maintenance loan is the money that is available to cover the cost of living. This is paid directly to you in instalments. What is important to remember with this loan is that the instalment dates are not a choice, they are an administrative element within the system and cannot be changed for your personal circumstances. This is something you will need to work around, so make a note of the dates and plan to budget carefully.

UK Students

All UK students are eligible to apply for both student fees loans and maintenance loans. However, there are variations between the UK nations about how this is done. For Scottish students studying in Scotland, make sure you access the Scottish government site rather than the UK government website, as the rules are slightly different (see BOX 3.9 for websites with up-to-date information).

Student Fees Loan

All UK students can apply to receive a loan that covers their tuition fees; these are the costs associated with doing your course. This loan is not contingent on age, financial situation, or any dependants you may have, and is only repayable once you earn a minimum amount following graduation, details of which can be found on the UK government website (website details provided in BOX 3.9).

It should be noted that there is no loan for fees for Scottish domiciled (resident) students studying an undergraduate degree, because the fees are automatically covered for free by the Student Awards Agency for Scotland (SAAS) in almost all cases. Students from the rest of the UK who study in Scotland have to pay student fees equivalent to the rest of the UK.

You don't start repaying your loan until the April *after* you graduate, for full-time students, or from the April four years after your course starts if you are part-time. However, you can opt to start paying back your loans before earning the baseline amount if you want to. Since you accrue interest each year from the point you receive your first loan, this is something to seriously consider if you can afford it once you graduate.

Maintenance Loans

Maintenance loans are intended to help with your living costs while you are at university. This loan is available for students in all UK nations, regardless of place of study, but the amount you can borrow might vary for Scottish students studying in Scotland. Look at the relevant government websites for more up-to-date details.

For the maintenance loan you need to apply and provide evidence of household income and dependents, since there are conditions attached to receiving it. For example, you cannot apply unless you are under 60, and if you are currently earning above a certain amount you will not get the maximum loan available, or possibly any at all. There are also different amounts available to those students living with parents and those living outside the family home, as well as whereabouts in the UK (London vs outside London), or the world, you are studying for each year of your degree.

The amount you receive is split into chunks throughout the year, paid in two instalments directly into your bank account. There are typically three payment points across the year, two of which will be associated with your course. For courses that start in September, the first instalment is usually made around September/October, and the second usually around January/February. For other courses that start later in the year, there is a payment date around April/May as well. Occasionally there are delays to the payments, particularly if you apply late, so make sure you factor that into your planning and ensure you have finances in place, if possible, to last you for the first two months of your course *before* you begin university.

You might also qualify for travel costs that you can apply for when you apply for your maintenance loan, although these will come in the form of a grant, so are not repayable. Only particular groups of students are able to access travel costs grants, so you should check the eligibility criteria carefully. You are also eligible for some additional study costs if you are a medical or dental student and are required to travel to clinical placements during your studies. There may be different rules for students who study in Scotland, Wales, and Ireland, and you should look at the student loans website for more information. As with all things related to finance, the information in this book is subject to change, so please make sure you look at the relevant government website and student loans website for the latest information.

EU Students

I got my student finance from my country (The Netherlands) which is sent monthly in portions; even though my university's rules were to pay off annual fees in a certain amount of instalments... I was able to contact the university and arrange a different payment plan to suit my student finance. They were very accommodating!

Davy

Prior to the 2020/21 academic year, EU students were eligible for 'Home' fees and had access to the student loans system. Due to the UK leaving the European Union on 1 January 2021, these rights have changed and students from the European Union no longer qualify for UK student loans and will be classified as overseas students, and subject to international fees for their courses.

My advice, for all EU students, is to look at university websites and see if there are any systems of finance and support that have been put in place where you want to study. You may find individual institutions are able to offer financial incentives for you to study with them, as many already have these in place for international students, although this is by no means a guarantee. Remember, we absolutely want you to come and study with us, so if you have questions about finance, check out the website of the university you wish to study at, and make sure you contact the International Student Support Team as well as the Finance Team (see BOX 3.2).

BOX 3.2 Sources of Financial Information for International and EU Students

Person/Service	Website
UK Council for International Student Affairs	https://www.ukcisa.org.uk/
Study UK—British Council	https://study-uk.britishcouncil.org/
Student Finance Support— University	
International Student Office—University	
Programme Leader	

International Students

> *If you're unsure how to budget for living on your own or this is your first time living alone then don't be afraid to ask for help from someone who you feel comfortable with or even from your university's financial team*
>
> **Eddy**

International students are not eligible for student loans within the UK unless they have been resident for three years already and have 'domiciled' status in the UK. You might also be eligible if you are a refugee or have been granted humanitarian protection, so it is worth investigating if this is the case for you. With the ever-changing rules around resident status in the UK, it is wise to check with the government website at the point you begin your studies; if you are not sure then contact the university Student Finance Team, who will be able to help.

All students from overseas who study in the UK should contact the university they will be studying at before they arrive to study, to ask if there are any grants and/or scholarships available to them within the university itself. While you might not be eligible for student loans, many universities offer incentives to international students, and these can be in the form of reduced accommodation fees or reduced course fees.

There are also many sources of financial support for international students and these can be found in BOX 3.2. You will need to complete some sections for your university, so find your local and university sources of support and make a note of them here.

The Link between Finances and Attendance

> *Familiarize yourself as soon as possible, as all the information you need to progress is on there.*
>
> **Anthony**

There is a link between your finances and your attendance, and this is not something that is widely publicized, mostly as it is expected that students will attend their courses. However, it is a really important consideration for all students attending university who rely on the student loans system in order to finance their studies. There are variations in how this is applied across universities of course, but ultimately the two are linked. The money you're given is a loan, not a grant, so you will have to pay it back at some point. If you are withdrawn from the course (either by the university or through choice) then you are going to have to pay back what you've borrowed; it's important to remember this.

If you don't attend classes then you may be given a variety of warnings, but ultimately if you continue not to attend classes, your place on your course will potentially be withdrawn and you will no longer be a student at university. What this means in financial terms is that you are expected to pay back any loans you may have taken out, and this is done immediately rather than through the normal loan repayment schedule that is future earnings dependent.

There is also the potential challenge of appealing the withdrawal decision and getting reinstated on your degree, and there may be the added difficulty that you no longer qualify for a student loan if you have been shown to be a student who is in 'poor standing'. In other words, if you were kicked out of university for not attending and then had to repay your loans, there is no guarantee you would ever get another loan for future courses. Remember, all loans have to be applied for and those details will be stored on government systems.

Sometimes university doesn't work out for students and they end up withdrawing voluntarily from their courses, for many reasons. If this happens to you, it's important to remember that you are still liable for a percentage of the loans you've received if this happens, and there are cut-off dates where this applies. In Table 3.1, I've listed what amount of your loans you are liable for, this means what you have to pay back, at each stage of the academic year.

If you do need to repay part of your loan and fees, then you should contact your Student Finance Team, even if you have left the university, as they will have the most up-to-date advice and can help you set up a payment plan if necessary.

If you take a temporary leave of absence (something covered in Chapter 13) then your payments from all student loans will be paused. This will happen automatically once you've completed the necessary

Table 3.1 The Percentage of Your Fees and Loans You're Liable for in Each Term

Stage of Year When Withdrawal Takes Place	Tuition Fees You Have to Pay Back	Maintenance Loan You Have to Pay Back
Term 1	25% of the whole tuition fee	100% of the instalment paid
Term 2	50% of the whole tuition fee	100% of the instalment paid
Term 3	100% of the whole tuition fee	100% of the instalment paid (for those courses where this is applicable)

procedures to pause your studies, as the university Student Finance Team will notify Student Finance England (or SAAS) and you will receive no payments until you officially restart your studies. You won't be immediately liable for repayment, as with a withdrawal, since your studies are only paused. But you do need to think about the impact the temporary loss of funding will have on you. Make sure you discuss the implications of pausing your studies and funding with the Student Finance Team at your university.

Getting a Part-Time Job

> Try not to sacrifice your future for your present . . . do just enough paid work to manage your finances, make sure your academic work comes first.
>
> **Anthony**

Many students work during their studies, for a variety of reasons, but some have no choice. You may already have a job that you now need to fit around your university studies. However, for many of you, getting a job will be something that you'll need to do in order to pay your bills, and if you're moving away to go to university, you'll need to do this once you relocate. All universities have careers services, and you will probably find they are well equipped to help new students find part-time employment, with the added bonus of workshops and sessions around how to apply, write applications, and develop your interview skills. Sometimes the Student Union supports students in getting employment, so ask what support is on offer.

Your university lecturers will understand it may be necessary for you to work while you study, so if you need to try and move some classes because of particular work schedules then discuss this with your lecturers (something that is covered in Chapter 4).

41

If you are juggling studying with working then time management is going to be a very important skill to develop. Make sure you read the section on time management in Chapter 8. If need be, talk to your employer about the hours you are contracted to do and whether restructuring your shift pattern around your university timetable is something they can accommodate. It may be that you can get extra shifts during university holidays, which is beneficial for both you and your employer. The first step is always to have a discussion with your supervisor or manager.

The goal of a part-time job is to generate enough income to cover your bills. It can be very tempting to take on extra shifts to get extra money, however this can sometimes come at the expense of your studies as it can result in missed classes, not having enough time to complete work to the best of your ability, and exhaustion. You need to find a balance with your part-time job as far as possible, doing enough so that you have sufficient funds to finance your life, but not overworking so that you penalize your own studies.

There can be significant pressure from employers, who are not always sympathetic to the demands of university courses. However, it is important to remember that being open and honest with your employer is a good first step, and ensuring you have a sit-down meeting with your line manager or supervisor before you start university will go a long way to ensuring a smooth working relationship. Take your timetable and any details you have about assignment/exam pinch points (think December/January, March–May) to highlight in advance the periods during which you may need to concentrate on your studies, and explain that you can do extra shifts over the summer to compensate.

And remember, if you are struggling with employer or workplace demands and you feel it is impacting your studies, you must contact your Personal Tutor and Programme Leader for advice, and make sure you read Chapters 6 and 13, so you are clear on what you need to do if you are struggling to meet assignment deadlines.

Students with Families and/or Caring Responsibilities

> If you are worried and feel as though you need help—don't be
> shy, speak up, no-one will judge you as you won't be in the boat
> alone.
>
> **Jamie**

For a great many students now, university is simply one extra thing to juggle in their busy lives. Financial considerations are always important, but when you have other people who depend on you to feed them and keep a roof over their heads, finances do become rather more of a priority. This is particularly the case when you've had to take a drop in hours in your job (or even quit altogether) in order to complete your course.

Before you start your course, make sure you have your finances in order and you know how you're going to pay your bills. We see many students leave university or take short breaks simply because of finances. It's always a good idea to plan for the unexpected, and making the assumption that there will be a financial struggle at one point during your studies means you can prepare for that early.

I recommend recording your finances in a spreadsheet. Write down the earnings you receive from any job/s you have (or how much you are entitled to in benefits from the various sources), the potential input from your student maintenance loan and any bursaries or scholarships you are entitled to, and then work out how much it all is per month. Then, make a list of your monthly outgoings: food, bills (utilities, broadband, council tax, if applicable, etc.), rent/mortgage, direct debits or standing orders for any other services or products, and the necessary outgoings for your family and yourself.

Now analyse the results. If the amount you have coming in is less than your outgoings, then work out what is, and is not, important during your studies, and what you can, and can't, cut down on. Remember, a few years of cutting corners is worth it in the long run; a degree will widen your career options and hopefully lead to better finances in the future.

Discuss your finances as a household and/or family unit before you start university, go through your options and discuss ways in which you might need to budget during your course. Being open and honest about finances before you start your course will help you navigate the financial considerations/decisions that come with university study.

Estranged/Care-Experienced Students

Finance is such an important area for students who come from care estranged/experienced backgrounds . . . Look into what scholarships and bursaries are available to you being a care-experienced/ estranged student from your university or local authority

Eddy

Some students may come to university without any support from family, due to familial relationships having broken down, or because they have been looked after by the local authority care systems, or private fostering, during their lives. These students are working hard to further their education and create a better future for themselves, and many universities now consider this group of students separately when it comes to additional financial, social, and mental health support. Within your university there may well be a specific team set up to support students who are estranged from family, or who are care-experienced, so are without the typical support systems the majority of students have.

If you are in this position, the Care-Experienced Student Support Teams (they may have a variety of names, but the terms 'care-experienced', and 'estranged student' should be enough to find them on university websites) will be able to support you in all matters, inclusive of finance and accessing any university-specific bursaries that are open to you. BOX 3.3 provides space for you to note down the contact details of people who may be able to support you.

The National Office for Students considers this group of students a priority group, so there is a bursary available; the university support teams and your care workers can help you access this. Many universities start support for care-experienced and estranged students long before they enter university, many working with care

BOX 3.3 Estranged/Care-Experienced Student Sources of Support

Person/Service	Phone	Email/Website
Care-Experienced Students Support Team		
University Student Finance Team		
Welfare Support/Adviser		
Programme Leader		
Personal Tutor		
Another Lecturer I know/trust		
Care Worker		
Additional Support Worker		

workers to ensure support is available for students for the entirety of their university journey, from application to graduation and often beyond.

One national organization that many universities sign up to is NNECL—The National Network for the Education of Care Leavers (http://nnecl.org). Universities who have signed up to be members of this organization, committing to improve the experience of education for care experienced students, are displayed in a scrolling banner at the bottom of their website.

If you are under 25 years of age and are estranged or care-experienced, you are assessed as an independent student with Student Finance England. UCAS are also due to add this as a category of student before 2025 so that university support systems can be alerted during the process and support can be put in place as needed.

Additional financial and wrap-around care support may be available through the university you attend, this may include any or all of the following: accommodation support, moving costs/use of a van, technology bursaries, vacation period support, bursaries for post-graduate study (supported by the Office for Students, UK) and, of course, mental health support, covered in more detail within Chapter 7.

Finally, there are moves to include homeless, Gypsy/Traveller students, asylum seekers and refugees, and military personnel leavers within this package of support as they may also have similar challenges outside of university. There is a significant amount of consideration for 'non-traditional' students now, and the financial aspects of this are an important part of this support. If you do have questions about the support available for someone in your particular circumstances, or even if you qualify for this additional support, just ask the Student Finance Team at the university you wish to attend, or have just joined. Do not be afraid to ask for support, there is a large amount of help available.

Benefits and Bursaries: What Do You Qualify For?

> Don't be shy or embarrassed to ask for hardship funds if you need them. There isn't always someone who needs it more … It's for people like you too. Sometimes it goes unspent.
>
> Liz

There are grants available for all sorts of things at university. Gone are the days when university was the preserve of the wealthy, now we have a wide-range of students attending university, with a wide variety of financial situations to navigate. In this section I'll go through a range of financial support that is in place for national students across most parts of the UK. Some of these might be available to international students, but you will need to talk to your university Student Finance Team for more advice.

Council Tax Exemption

All students studying in the UK qualify for exemption from, or a reduction in, Council Tax. Council Tax is paid on all private residences in the UK, so if you live in private accommodation this is something you want to get in place right at the start of your course, or at the point you move in. The way to get this is to apply through your local council website. You will need confirmation of your status as a student, and you can get a letter from your university regarding this. Often your acceptance letter is insufficient, since councils want to make sure you have taken up your place and are a current student; universities are aware of this already so can provide you with a letter. Sometimes you can get a Council Tax exemption certificate when you enrol, either through asking at the Student Advice Point, or by printing one off from your Student Account. BOX 3.4 has details of who to contact to get a letter for council tax exemption.

You can get complete exemption from Council Tax if you live with other students in private accommodation. If you live with non-students then they are entitled to a 25% reduction in council tax, regardless of their income, as the single-person occupancy is applied to your property. You may also find your non-student adult house-mates/partner can also apply for additional reductions, and this can be discussed directly with staff at your local council offices.

Scholarships

Some universities have scholarship programmes that you can apply for, or sometimes get automatically due to personal circumstances. These tend to be specific pots of money that are classed as grants, which means you don't have to pay them back. There are also scholarships run by external organizations. For example, the Ministry of

BOX 3.4 Where to Get a Letter Stating You're a Current Student at University

Person/Service	Contact Number	Contact Email/ Website
Student Support		
Programme Leader		
School/Department Admin team		
Student Advice Point		
Welfare Support/Adviser		

Defence runs an Enhanced Learning Credits Scheme (ELCAS) that has run a Department for Education bursary scheme for veterans applying to particular courses.

Scholarships can be for all sorts of things: accommodation costs, university fees, cash bursaries, specialist equipment (more details below), or transport costs. They can either be set amounts of money or cover the full cost of items needed.

People who qualify for scholarships fall into a number of categories: lone/single parents, estranged students, students who come from a care-based background (care-experienced), or they could be available to all students at a particular level (e.g. local travel passes are often available to all first year and foundation students). However, they are often available to full-time students only, so this is something to check with the finance team at the university you attend.

Those scholarships you apply for will ask for proof that you qualify, and the details of this will be on your university website. You should expect to have to provide evidence in the form of identity, residence, income, expenditure, and home situation.

To find details of all scholarships connected with your university, you should find the details (use BOX 3.5) and contact someone to discuss your options.

BOX 3.5 Scholarship Information at My University

Person/Service	Phone	Email/Website
Scholarship Team		
Student Advice Point		
Welfare Support/Adviser		
University Student Finance Team		

Training Bursaries

Some courses have bursaries attached to them in order to attract applicants, often in fields defined as having a shortage of professional staff, such as Nursing and Medicine. These could include training grants, additional grants for dependants, travel bursaries, regional incentive payments, and so on.

For individual professions with these bursaries, you are likely to be sent this information when you register on your course, and if you have specific questions then these should be directed to your university Student Finance Team. It should be noted that these are grants/bursaries and are therefore non-repayable as long as you complete your course.

Students with Disabilities

There are grants available for those students who have a registered disability, be that a physical disability, a long-term condition, a mental health condition, or a learning disability such as dyslexia. These are called DSA—Disabled Students' Allowance. The DSA can help with the purchase of specialist equipment, for example a computer or associated specialist software, travel costs, personal support, non-medical helpers, and associated costs of studying. Some universities do not sign up to the DSA scheme and instead run their own in-house system. Check out what your university has in place.

Those who cannot access the DSA are EU students, students doing a course that lasts less than one year, and those students getting support through other schemes, such as the NHS Disabled Students' Allowance. There is, however, no age limit on the DSA.

The DSA, or equivalent, can be applied for through your university Student Finance Team, but the Well-being teams and Student Support Services are typically well versed in the details of these particular

BOX 3.6 Contacts for Students Applying for the Disabled Students' Allowance (DSA)

Person/Service	Phone	Website/Email
Well-being Team		
Student Advice Team		
University Student Finance Team		

grants, so may be able to assist you in these applications. Since most students who can apply for the DSA, or equivalent, need to contact the Student Support Teams anyway, the Support Teams should be your first port of call once you have registered on your course as they will be able to point you in the right direction and support you getting access to the support elements you need to complete your course. BOX 3.6 lists the contacts you will need, so make sure you write down the contact details and get in touch as soon as you've registered on your course.

Benefits

Everybody's finances are different.
Milo

There are a variety of means-tested financial support available to UK students, and students in vulnerable groups, for example lone/single parents, students with disabilities, or those deemed unable to work. Your university Student Finance Team will have all the details of what you are, or are not, eligible for in terms of benefits, but the Citizens Advice Bureau is also an excellent source of support (see BOX 3.7).

BOX 3.7 Sources of Benefits Information

Person/Source of Support	Phone	Website/Email
University Student Finance Team		
Citizens Advice Bureau		https://www.citizensadvice.org.uk/
Turn2Us		https://www.turn2us.org.uk/
Gingerbread (for lone/single parents)		https://www.gingerbread.org.uk/information/benefits-tax-credits-and-universal-credit/if-youre-planning-to-study/benefits-youre-studying/

However, something that you do need to be aware of is that maintenance loans are classed as income, even if they aren't classed as taxable income. This means that part (not all) of your maintenance loan will be used to calculate any benefits you might be eligible for. This is important information to be aware of when discussing your financial options.

Adult Dependants and Childcare Grants

Students with family members who are dependent on them financially can get access to a variety of support packages within the financial systems of the UK.

If you have a co-habiting partner or spouse who is financially dependent on you then you may be eligible to apply for a grant. This features within the Scottish system as well, so if you are funded through the SAAS, the Students Awards Agency Scotland, then you may be eligible for a Dependent's Allowance.

Juggling parenting duties alongside work and university commitments can be a source of stress. Fortunately, for those of you with children not yet at school, there are also grants you may be eligible for that can help with childcare costs. If you are a lone/single parent, have a student partner, or have a partner unable to work or on a low income, you may be eligible for support for childcare costs. All childcare must be through OFSTED-registered providers, and there are maximum amounts available, but this is a really useful source of financial support if you are worried about childcare costs while you are at university. One thing to note is that often the funded nursery places are only available in term times linked to the local schools. This means that, because university does not align with these term dates, you may need to find additional costs for some weeks of the year (typically half-terms).

There are, however, some catches with the childcare financial support. If you are claiming Working Tax Credit or University Credit, you are automatically not eligible for childcare support costs. Likewise, if you are a Scottish student studying at a UK university, you would not qualify for this financial support.

Parent's Learning Allowances

Sometimes there are grants available to support students who are parents to manage study costs alongside raising their children. These are fixed amounts and classed as non-repayable grants. In Scotland, students who are lone/single parents are also entitled to something called the Lone Parent Grants if they are funded by SAAS. Lone/single parents in English and Welsh universities might find they can apply for a fee reduction through their university. For details of these and how to apply, contact your university Student Finance Team.

Free School Meals

For those of you with children at school, or about to go to school, you can receive free school meals if you fit into one of the following categories:

1. You get Child Tax Credit but don't qualify for Working Tax Credit
2. You get Universal Credit

Importantly, in this instance, your student loans do not count towards the calculation that is made, as they are non-taxable income. So you can apply for free school meals without worrying that your student loan will suddenly be taken into account and you'll lose access to them.

Hardship Funds

Sometimes life can throw a curveball that can severely impact financial status for students, putting them at risk of dropping out of their studies simply because they have no money to continue. This is obviously a situation that can be very distressing to the students involved, and hopefully it will never happen to you. While we can't solve financial problems there is a safety net in the form of a hardship fund available for you to apply to.

These funds can be accessed through a process of application, and you will need evidence of income and costs for an assessment of your situation to be made. There are also likely to be priority groups for accessing this particular fund, for example students with children, students incapable of working, and those in their final year of studies.

Make sure you complete BOX 3.8 below so that if you do end up in a difficult situation you know who to contact for support.

BOX 3.8 Who to Contact When You Experience Unexpected Financial Difficulties

Person/Service	Phone	Email/Website
Programme Leader		
Personal Tutor		
Another Lecturer I know/trust		
Student Finance Team		
Welfare Support/Adviser		

What you will also find is that there are administrative things we can do to support you, for example putting in place something called a 'Leave of Absence'. You will find more details about this in Chapter 13.

How Not to Spend All Your Loan at Once!

> My top tip for any prospective student starting would be to set out a budgeting plan [and] if you have any money left over from income, bursaries, student loan etc., try to save some for a rainy day if you can, you never know when you may need it.
>
> *Eddy*

Many students get their maintenance loans and become a little overwhelmed by the amount of money they have at one time. We find that most mature students don't have this issue since they're already aware of the concept of budgeting and how long money has to last. But for younger students not used to managing their finances independently, it can be an intoxicating start to the academic year and they often spend their newfound wealth on new computers, nights out, gadgets, clothes, and more. Then it gets to October and they realize they need to live on baked beans for the next three months as they don't have any money. The money you receive is intended to last you four months—you therefore need to make it last that long.

Budgeting Your Maintenance Loan

> Pay your rent first!
> **Sarah**

Making your finances stretch across all your expenses is a challenge for the majority of students. There is lots of advice out there, here is mine.

 VANESSA'S TOP TIPS

for making your money stretch further

> Get a budgeting app, make plans, and don't splurge.
> **Daisy**

- Work out how much money you have coming in and how much you have going out.

  Once you know what your resources are, you can plan how to spread your income evenly so you don't fall short. If you forget to account for rent and food bills, for example, you're going to run into difficulties very quickly. A good method of doing this is to separate your list into 'essential', such as rent and food, and 'non-essential', such as haircuts and cinema tickets. Make sure your essential expenses are paid first, then look at what you have available for non-essential expenses.

- Look at your existing payments and direct debits.

Are you getting the best deal on everything you currently pay for? It's maybe worth looking at your phone contracts, paid-TV contracts, subscriptions, and any other outgoings you have regularly coming out of your account. List your priorities and then adjust accordingly. If you end up cancelling a subscription or two, try and remember that it's just for a short while, and your priority is getting a degree. And if you want to keep the subscriptions, don't complain about having to do extra shifts at work or eating beans for a week!

- Look for all available student discounts.

Welcome to student life, where paying full price is often not needed. Check out the NUS (National Union of Students) Student Discount page, for a big list of discounts. You will also find student discount cards available through your own university Students' Union.

- Download a budgeting app.

There are loads of apps out there to help you budget; have a look at and see which is the best fit for you. Some universities even have their own app available, which you will be able to find details about on their Student Finance pages.

- Consider getting a student account.

The condition of most student accounts is that your maintenance loan is paid directly into them. However, this then gives you access to an agreed overdraft, which can really help while you're a student; although be careful of going over this, as there are often steep charges associated with going over your overdraft limit, or there may even be a stop on payments so your regular standing orders and direct debits will bounce and this could cause additional problems. Keep in mind that an overdraft is for emergencies, not every day use. With student accounts, look around for the best deals and get the account that works for you. Sometimes there are even student discount cards, gifts, and railcards available as incentives—look at what works for you. Remember, an overdraft is borrowed money, you will have to pay it back.

- Download a banking app.

  Much like budgeting apps, banking apps can help you keep in touch with how much money you have available to you at any one time, including any payments that are due to go out. Some banks are run on an app basis now, others have an app associated with the regular accounts. Many of the big banking names also now have budgeting tools within their apps. If you know how much you have available, and how long it has to last, it can make it easier to budget.

- Consider setting up a standing order for yourself.

  If you are concerned that you will spend all your available money quickly, consider setting up a standing order from your student account, where your maintenance loan will be deposited, to another account, either existing or new, that you can use as a 'spending' account. You can then effectively give yourself a weekly allowance. This enables you to regulate your own spending and ensures that your maintenance loan lasts as long as it's needed.

- Set up a savings account.

  Regular saving is something we all know we're supposed to do, but often when you're working on a tight budget it can feel like you haven't got enough money to save. You may already have savings, or you may be new to opening a savings account. But saving a little of your maintenance loan for a rainy day is a really sensible thing to do, because you never know when you might lose shifts at work, have a sudden expense, or any other situation where you suddenly need to find some money quickly. A savings account that you can access quickly is a great idea while you're a student. You might even find that there are saving options available with your bank that allow you to save a tiny bit at a time, where you don't notice. For example, there are several banks and accounts that have a scheme whereby you can sign up to automatically save the 'change' up to the nearest pound every time you make a payment on your card. This small saving of pennies can lead to quickly saving a surprising amount.

Technology and Your Course

Companies are aware of when student loans drop. I went without a laptop for my first term of my undergraduate degree and soon realized I needed one. I decided to wait until my second student loan came in to get one which meant I got my laptop for £399 when it was previously up for £599. The extra £200 went a long way!

Nicole

Universities were already well on the way to undergoing a technical revolution before the COVID-19 pandemic; now that pace has increased. You are going to need to get appropriate technical equipment for your course if you wish to gain a degree, and this is now an important consideration for going to university.

Getting a suitable computer for your studies is essential; for most of you this will be a laptop that you can access materials and create your work on. You will need something that will cope with the demands of your course, but you also need to balance this with your income and any additional financial pressures you're under.

Look at all the options available to you, but don't be swayed by the well-known brands. There are some great computers available at a fraction of the price of the big names. A good computer doesn't cost much, at least not for the basic demands of university life.

Carefully consider the promotions and make sure you read the reviews and ask the tech experts in stores near you to find one that works for you. Remember, you will probably need to download additional software at some point during your degree, so make sure you get a laptop that can do that. If you're not sure, talk to the tech experts in your local store and ask them. You might also find your new lecturers will have plenty of advice on what to get (and what to avoid!).

Digital Poverty

During the COVID-19 pandemic, we became increasingly aware that many of our students fell into a category called 'Digital Poverty' and relied on university computing provision to complete their course. When campuses were forcibly closed, the lack of access to computers became a significant barrier to completing work for some students. This wasn't limited to those in low socio-economic groups either; this was students from all walks of life, national and international. While smartphones can do a great deal these days, and many universities use systems that have associated apps that students can conduct their studies on, they are no substitute for a full-size laptop or computer. Apart from the fact smartphones have relatively small screens, if the smartphone model is out-of-date, then it can't always get the latest software update, meaning some apps don't work at all. All students need to have much better computing provision to complete their degrees.

Most universities have free computing facilities, often available 24 hours a day in some places. Make sure that if you do not have suitable computing equipment at home, you make use of your time in university and ensure you access the facilities provided for free.

Sometimes it might be the case that the cost of getting to university is prohibitive, and the extra money needed to come in to study on a non-teaching day is something you can't afford. Or you might have to work at home due to childcare issues and/or access to local work. There are many reasons why students can't just come into university on days off, evenings, and weekends, so if this applies to you, talk to the Student Finance Team and discuss what options you have for bursaries and funding the technical side of your studies. You might be able to borrow a laptop for the duration of your studies, or your university might have a scheme in place to gift you a suitable laptop or device.

A Note on Keeping Up To Date with Financial Information

Rules around fees and loans are ever changing and can be relatively complex depending on your exact situation.

Liz

Obviously, things can change rapidly in the field of finance, and there may well be some minor changes during the course of your studies, and indeed between the publication of this book and you reading through the content. I've included a list of great resources here for you (see BOX 3.9) so that you can check any information and ensure you are fully aware of your financial rights and what you have access to while you're at university. I've put a blank space at the bottom though, because your own university will always have the most up-to-date information for your course, and they should always be your first port of call when you're needing information about financial matters.

BOX 3.9 A List of Resources with Up-To-Date Information

Source of Financial Information	Website
Your University Student Finance Team	
UCAS	https://www.ucas.com/sfe
Student Loans Company	https://www.gov.uk/government/organisations/student-loans-company
Student Finance UK	https://www.gov.uk/student-finance
Student Finance Scotland	https://www.mygov.scot/apply-student-loan
Student Awards Agency Scotland	https://www.saas.gov.uk/
Which (great for regional variations)	https://www.which.co.uk/money/university-and-student-finance/student-finance/complete-guide-to-student-loans-and-tuition-fees-anskp9q9qw0p

A Final Word

> Don't be afraid to reach out for guidance and support from your lecturers or/and other university staff
>
> **Eddy**

Finances are a tricky subject; while you're studying, they are often going to be a balancing act. Getting fully informed and planning ahead is vital while you're at university. Budgeting is a key part of managing your finances so you don't end up in difficulties and/or struggling to feed yourself and others who depend on you.

There is a lot of support at university, and finances are no exception. A phrase from where I live is 'shy bairns get nowt', and this definitely applies to finance and asking for support. If you need financial support, don't be embarrassed; university is hugely expensive now, so please just ask for advice and help if you need it. And remember, your student loans really are tied to your attendance, so turn up to class!

www.oup.com/he/parson1e

Visit the online resources where you will find additional materials including guides on time management, financial planning and budgeting, mindfulness and mental health, hints and tips, as well as all the tables from the book.

Chapter 4

HOW A DEGREE ACTUALLY WORKS

Why This Chapter Is Important

- Understanding how a degree works in the modern era will help you navigate your academic journey.
- Knowing where to find information, and who to ask, is an important factor in increasing your confidence during your academic journey.
- This chapter covers the fundamentals of your academic journey, including grading and what happens if you don't pass assignments.

> *Just because your first year MAY not count towards your degree doesn't mean that it's not worth doing well. It's intended to be a leveller, a chance to develop, take a chance, and find out how to succeed at university. Use the opportunity wisely and as a chance to improve and experiment.*
>
> Liz

While it's important to get finances in place and make friends on the course, it's also very important to understand how your degree works so that you can get on with the studying required to complete it. There are a wide variety of degrees available now, but most have the same basic structure. Any differences will typically be in duration, how long the course lasts, and format (how the degree is delivered). For example, while the majority of degrees last three years, Scottish degrees last four years, the Open University runs its degrees part-time over a long period of time, and some universities are now exploring how to condense degrees into just two years or moving to part-time options. Some programmes are outside this standardization and run in a different format.

All of this will be clearly provided on the websites and within university policy, so read the information your university provides about your course carefully so you know how your degree timeline works. Most degrees will have a time limit attached to them; this means that you have a certain length of time to complete them. This will be something written into university policy, so check your individual university regulations and any student handbooks and programme regulations you have access to. If you're not sure, contact your programme leader.

Term Dates

Check term dates well in advance and arrange childcare/work AROUND these.

Ebony

Your year at university will typically look similar to the terms you had a college or school; however, the year is usually split into two semesters at university. You will find that most (not all) universities run their classes across a semester, with exam weeks at the end of each. Some universities still run on a term structure, and this is something that will be clear on the publicized term dates.

Many courses (such as Nursing), however, run throughout the year, as they include placements. And sometimes courses have multiple start points that change things up a bit—most students start in September, but courses can start in January or April as well. Online-only courses can start at many points throughout the year.

Your university will already have sorted out the term dates well in advance and they will be available on the website, along with when your vacation periods are, so find those and put them in BOX 4.1. Make sure that you only book holidays or flights back to your home country within the scheduled vacation periods: you are expected to be in classes during term unless there is an emergency.

There are alternative tables to complete in the appendix to this book, as well as the digital accompaniment to this book; pick the one which matches the course dates for your university and complete it so you have all the dates you need in an easy-access location.

BOX 4.1 Term Dates

	Start	End
Semester 1		
Winter vacation		
Winter exam period		
Semester 2		
Spring vacation		
Summer exam period		

Timetables

> Screenshot your timetable the first few weeks of a new semester and save it as your background! That was the best tip I ever had! Saved me wandering round confused all the time!
>
> **Cara**

Your timetable will usually be located online; you'll be able to access it via the university website, and often through a university app. Make sure you know how to access it and then make sure you check it the night before classes. Each of your classes will have a code and name for the module, a code for the room and building, plus the week numbers. Once you crack the code it's easy to understand. Early on, if you get stuck just ask a member of staff or go to the Help Desk. Often this is something that's highlighted in Freshers' Week Programme talks (see Chapter 5), so these are especially important to attend. If you don't understand your timetables then ask your tutors or lecturers, or go to the university Help Desk. They're usually very straightforward, but with lots of numbers and codes on, they can get confusing when you first start university.

It is your responsibility to get to class, so make sure you know where and when those classes are and the most sensible way of getting from one class to another. If you're not sure about where your classes are being held, take yourself on a tour around all the rooms listed on your timetable, ideally with some of the friends you made in Freshers' Week.

Most students will find that exams form part of their degree assessment because sometimes we do need to find out what students know without the help of books. There are likely to be two big exam periods during the year, although some modules may have smaller exams/tests as you go through.

You will typically find your exam timetable in the same place as your timetable, online and potentially via a university app as well (if your university uses them), although the exam timetable may be communicated separately in some universities. You may not be told directly when your exams are; typically, you'll be told that there will be exams and then asked to check your timetable. We will always tell you where you need to look though. Always check your timetable first, and if the information is not there *then* go and talk to your Module Leader (sometimes called other things, such as Module Convenor). We also have something called 'resit' (or 'referred/deferred') exam periods, where students who didn't sit the exams can take them (there are lots of reasons this can happen). The dates for these will be university-specific, so if you want to be prepared, ask your Programme Leader (sometimes called Programme Director or Course Leader).

For all key module sessions and exams I recommend putting them into your phone calendar (along with all your assignment deadlines) as it will alert you to the fact that you've got a class and/or deadline coming up. If you prefer a paper diary, then get an academic year one and put everything in there. Use post-it notes and coloured pens so that things stand out. We'll let you know if a class needs moving, so checking the online timetable regularly is important too.

Staff on Your Course

Don't be afraid to talk to people.
Sarah

There are many staff who will support you on your academic journey, and in BOX 4.2 you'll find a table to complete with their contact details. It's the academic staff (your lecturers and tutors) who you will interact

BOX 4.2 University Staff Contact Details

Staff Role	Email Address	Location	Staff Availability Hours
Programme Leader			
Module Leader(s)			
Personal Tutor			
Study Skills			
Help Desk			

with the most, and this is the team you need to be really familiar with. Before university there are teachers, or tutors, and sometimes you saw a Head of School or Head Teacher. Within universities there are many different staff, and with different roles on your course. Knowing who is responsible for what is important (see Chapter 2). I've set out these roles and how they relate to each other in my Academic Family Tree (see Figure 4.1). It is important to remember that this is a general representation, so individual universities might show some variation on this. What is important for you to remember is that individual staff might have more than one role, so it might be that the same person is both your Programme Leader *and* your Module Leader.

Personal Tutors

If you feel that something is not right, please go and tell someone.

Emma

Figure 4.1 The Academic Family Tree

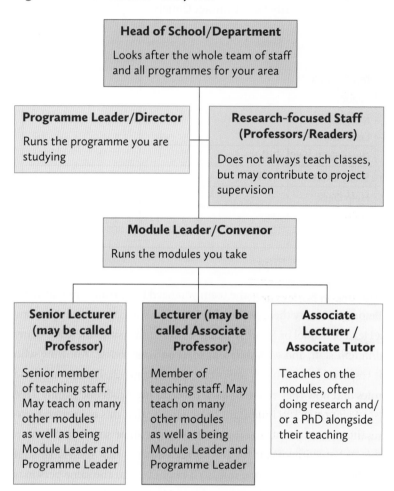

Head of School/Department

Looks after the whole team of staff and all programmes for your area

Programme Leader/Director

Runs the programme you are studying

Research-focused Staff (Professors/Readers)

Does not always teach classes, but may contribute to project supervision

Module Leader/Convenor

Runs the modules you take

Senior Lecturer (may be called Professor)

Senior member of teaching staff. May teach on many other modules as well as being Module Leader and Programme Leader

Lecturer (may be called Associate Professor)

Member of teaching staff. May teach on many other modules as well as being Module Leader and Programme Leader

Associate Lecturer / Associate Tutor

Teaches on the modules, often doing research and/ or a PhD alongside their teaching

Alongside the core staff outlined in the Academic Family Tree (see Figure 4.1) are your Personal Tutors. These may or may not be taken from your academic team, but the emphasis on personal tutoring is something that has expanded in recent years, particularly in response to the COVID-19 pandemic when a great many more students needed considerable support.

Personal Tutors are there to support you during your studies, enabling a personal perspective to be taken on your academic study, as well as supporting your personal and professional development. They will help keep you focused and will be a source of support when needed, a person to ask questions of, and an advocate for your case when needed. Often Personal Tutors are allocated on a whole-degree level, but sometimes they may change depending on degree structure and staff turnover. If you are struggling with anything at any point, your Personal Tutor is one of the first people to contact.

Study Skills and Support Staff

> Use drop-in sessions and help offered by tutors where and when needed. they are there to help!
>
> **Chantelle**

You will also find a whole host of support staff available to help you with your course, from technical support staff to those in the library. Throughout this text I've referred to them where needed, but the group of staff I need to highlight here are those staff who support you with your study skills. These could be specialized staff, academic tutors, and librarians, for example, but there will always be staff, and resources, dedicated to supporting you with your academic work. Many universities have dedicated teams who offer support and resources to help with the development of key study skills. Sometimes, these teams work across all disciplines and other times there will be subject-specific teams that operate from a specific department. Often, they will cover skills such as writing, referencing, and time management; more specific skills such as maths/statistics support are sometimes covered, although these are typically supported within individual programme teams.

This is a hugely important area of your study and it's important to remember a degree is not just about the acquisition of knowledge, it is also about communicating your understanding of that knowledge. This is where study skills come in, enabling you to develop your writing and academic skills throughout your degree so that you can clearly demonstrate your knowledge and achieve the degree commensurate with that knowledge.

Help Desks

> They [the lecturers] would rather you ask [questions] than not ask and struggle.
>
> **Milo**

We know you will have questions during your degree, so most universities will have central points where students can go and ask any of the myriad of questions they have each year. These might be called something specific (e.g. Gateway) or just 'Help Desk', but these points will be your central point for asking questions related to your time at university. Often, they are located somewhere central and are staffed throughout the day, both in term time and often in vacation time as well.

Help Desks are not limited to academic queries, they can point you in the direction of all university services, tutors, timetables, programme contacts, policies, documents, or processes, student cards; the list goes on. If you do have a question and aren't sure who will know the answer, the Help Desks are where you go. They are your go-to source for directions to all the help you need during your degree.

Reading Weeks

> *Everyone seems to think they are for a week off. They aren't, but they ARE a break from normal classes and . . . a fantastic opportunity to catch up on some reading.*
> **Kaylie**

Some (not all) universities have reading weeks, and during reading weeks there is usually a break in classes—no lectures, seminars, or other practical sessions. The intention is to provide you with a week to catch up on reading and taking notes. It is crucial to remember that reading weeks are for working, they are not a holiday and should not be treated as such. They are a university week but without classes—take advantage of this and get ahead in your studies.

Occasionally, reading weeks coincide with half-term, so those with childcare responsibilities have an additional challenge to navigate during those weeks. It's important to remember that universities cannot take account of all variations of school term dates, as this is disruptive to your own studies. Sometimes dates of reading weeks and half-terms don't coincide, which may be a welcome break for those who are parents, although it can make the half-term week difficult to juggle. Difficult as it is to negotiate university while you have childcare responsibilities, having the time to catch up in peace and quiet is incredibly useful—so take advantage of this when you get it! Planning ahead will serve you well, get school holidays and readings weeks into your diary at the start of the year, and plan for any extra childcare you will need to juggle.

What you must, ideally, not do during reading weeks, is take on too many extra shifts at work. Financial challenges are a significant part of doing a degree now (see Chapter 4), and we understand that most students are navigating their work lives as well as their student lives (and family lives). While we all understand the challenges you face, reading weeks are incredibly important for you to catch up with reading, ensure you are happy you know the work covered so far, and check that you have enough time to complete your assignments.

Reading weeks are not a break so tempting as it might be to do extra shifts, go on holiday with the kids, have some downtime, try to resist and make time to complete the work you need to do. Learning and understanding takes time; make sure you give yourself this.

Stages of Your Degree

> The better you do in the lower years, the better position you're in for the years that formally count. The later years might seem less of a jump if you do more than you need earlier on.
>
> **Faye**

We'll start with the basic structure. Your degree will last a set number of years, between three to four years for most students, unless you're doing a part-time or non-traditional degree structure. The vast majority of students will complete their degrees within this time frame, without any significant problems.

The years are called Stages AND Levels—which can be confusing at first. It's the result of several systems existing at once, so we now simply map across from one to the other.

The National Curriculum in schools works on Levels (GCSE is level 2, A level is level 3), but historically universities had Stages. The final year of secondary school is Year 13, and this is Level 3, along with many BTEC and NVQ courses, and of course all Access courses. Your university may use Stages or Levels or, like my university, use both. Even staff occasionally get confused so don't worry if you don't grasp it right away. In Table 4.1a and 4.1b there is a translation code for you, to help you understand what your lecturers are talking about.

The Scottish higher education system is slightly different in that the degrees are typically four years long. This is partly due to the Scottish education system being slightly different from the rest of the UK. Year 13 (Level 3 in England/Wales) is actually very similar to Level 7 in a Scottish university. Very occasionally, students from England/Wales can enter a Scottish degree in Level 8 (year 2) if their grades are high enough. However, this is an exceptional case, and most students will do a four-year course if studying in Scotland.

Courses at universities in Ireland can be three to four years, depending on the subject and institution. There are some courses that last a lot longer, for example medicine and veterinary science both last five years plus additional postgraduate training.

Table 4.1a Stage-Level-Year Translation—English and Welsh Universities

Stage 0—Foundation Year	Foundation Year/Level 3
Stage 1—First Year	Level 4 (undergraduate year 1)
Stage 2—Second Year	Level 5 (undergraduate year 2)
Stage 3—Third Year	Level 6 (undergraduate year 3—graduation year)
Stage 4—Masters Year	Level 7 (Masters Level)

Table 4.1b Year-Level Translation—Scottish Universities

First Year	Level 7 (undergraduate year 1)
Second Year	Level 8 (undergraduate year 2)
Third Year	Level 9 (undergraduate year 3)
Fourth Year	Level 10 (undergraduate year 4—graduation year)
Masters Year	Level 11 (Masters Level)

However, the vast majority of courses in the UK are between three and four years, or equivalent in part-time/non-traditional time.

Up until the final two years of your degree, we cover a basic grounding in your subject which ensures that everyone has the same level of knowledge going into the 'Honours' degree section. The most important part of your degree (usually the final two years) are your 'Honours' years, and these are the years which count towards your final degree. You will take some core modules (these are modules that everyone has to take), but often you get the opportunity to shape your degree to your personal interests and take a range of more specialist options modules, so it looks a bit more like what you enjoy.

How Grades Work and How They're Different from Pre-University Marking

The lecturers know who works hard.
Miles

Pre-university the grading structures have changed several times and within individual schools and colleges there are variations again. You may have been used to the A/B/C system, or you may have had a number system where 1 is low and 9+ is high. But you may also just have had percentages on your work to show your performance. At university we have had a consistent system for a very long time, and to ensure consistency across all degrees in the UK we use the same metrics at all universities.

For most universities, the criteria to pass an assignment and/or module is 40%. Yes, you want to get more than that and I'm sure you will. However, it is good to be aware of what our minimum requirement is. The minimum of 40% is equivalent to a 3rd class mark; less than that

Table 4.2 Degree Classifications

Percentage Mark	Degree Boundary	Letter-Grading Equivalent
70+	1st class mark	A
60–69%	Upper 2nd class mark	B
50–59%	Lower 2nd class mark	C
40–49%	3rd class mark	D
0–39%	Fail	E - Fail

and you have failed the assignment and/or module. We'll come to what happens in that situation shortly. In Table 4.2 there is a breakdown of the grade boundaries with equivalents for the letter-grading system you may be used to. There are no number-grading equivalents, as those relate more to GCSE so do not map onto degree grades.

Understanding the Criteria for Passing Assignments

> The best thing is start as you mean to go on, come to every lesson prepared and take notes and you'll see your uni life gets easier.
>
> **Alex**

Sounds easy enough to get 40%, right? Technically yes in your first year, but you have to make sure you meet what are known as *Learning Objectives* in order to pass every assignment, and if you don't meet those you won't get 40%.

Learning Objectives are a list of things that you are expected to understand (knowledge) and be able to do (skills) by the time you have completed the module. Your assignments will cover some or all of these learning objectives, depending on how many assignments per module you have. If you have one assignment, then all the learning objectives will need to be met in that single assignment, but if there are multiple assignments then the learning objectives are often split between these, so you focus on a few at a time.

It is really important to meet these objectives; even if you write the best essay ever, if you've not answered the question or used relevant literature (i.e. if you went off topic and used Google as your go-to resource) (pro tip—don't do either of these things!) then you haven't met the learning outcomes so cannot pass the assignment.

Do you know where to find your learning objectives for each module? You should find them in the module handbook, or on the Virtual Learning Environment (VLE), and your lecturers will often put them on assignment briefs and lecture slides.

When we're marking your work we use a set of marking criteria. Some universities have general ones, so-called generic criteria, that work for the vast majority of assignments, with unique assignments having their own form of criteria validated. Then some universities have different criteria for different assignments. All these criteria should be easily available to you and your lecturers will direct you to them.

Learning objectives and marking criteria are really useful things to keep a record of, as they tell you what you need to do in order to pass your assignments and learn the things we cover. We create learning objectives carefully so we can carefully scaffold your learning goals over your degree. Each learning objective is structured according to your year of study and specified at module level. They tell you what we are expecting you to achieve within your modules, and what you need to do in order to pass your assignments. Ignore them at your peril! They're always listed in your module and programme guides, and typically on your assignment briefs as well. In BOX 4.3 write down where you can find the learning objectives and marking criteria that your work will be marked against, and make sure you tick when you have downloaded a copy for your records.

BOX 4.3 Marking Criteria

Module Name	Learning Objectives	Recorded/ Downloaded	Marking Criteria (specialist/ generic)	Recorded/ Downloaded

How You Progress to the Next Year of Study

> Plan and prepare. Two words I failed to stick by during 1st year and the first half of 2nd year and by god it showed! The less you do at first the more you have to do at a later date!
>
> **Bethany**

Quite simply, you have to pass all your modules with a minimum of 40%. As not all modules have just one assignment, we look at the combination of these marks to determine your overall grade.

How we do this is going to be set out in your Module Handbooks/ Guides, so read those carefully.

An Academic Board confirms marks from all assignments and decides which students progress to the next year of study. All marks are provisional until they have gone to an Academic Board, which is typically made up of all your lecturers, plus any additional senior staff in the department. There are also External Examiners, who are academics from other universities that effectively double-check that the marking is all accurate and consistent. All lecturers do this; it ensures consistency between universities and ensures that a degree holds value and equivalence across all institutions.

While most of the time we look at the overall module grade, some universities will expect you to pass every assignment within the module as well (i.e. it won't be enough to get an average of 40% if one of the assignments was a fail), something called a Programme-Specific Requirement. So, check your Programme Handbook for the latest information that applies to your course and make sure you're clear on what you need to do to succeed (see BOX 4.4).

Each year you will take 120 credits (in most institutions, some have different numbers of credits, for example the Open University use a 160 credits per year structure). However many credits you're taking, you have to pass all of them with a minimum of 40%. If you get *almost* 40% in a module, you might find that you're compensated in that module (the Academic Board determines that you've met the learning outcomes for that module), so that is listed as a pass. If this rule applies where you study, it will be at the Academic Board's discretion—always try your best to pass all assignments on every module you take.

Making sure you know when all your deadlines are is crucial. We'll cover time management in Chapter 6; for now, make sure you have a note of all your deadlines so you know what is coming during this year (BOX 4.5).

BOX 4.4 Key Module and Programme Information

My programme says I need to pass every module with:	
My programme handbook is located:	

My module assignments contribute this much to my overall mark for that module

Module	Assignment	% Contribution to the Module

BOX 4.5 Your Deadlines

Module	Assignment	Deadline

Extensions

> Ask for extensions ... especially if you are really struggling with illnesses, sick children or any emergencies that happen ... life can throw some really hard challenges at you.
>
> **Emma**

We know life can sometimes impact on your work, so if you are genuinely struggling to meet a deadline, then you should talk to your lecturers. Your Module Leader is often the person who is permitted to grant you an extension so that you can still submit your work. Your Module Leader may, or may not, be your tutor, so don't assume that all tutors will be able to grant extensions, as that isn't the case. In many universities, a central team will handle extensions, and this is something that tutors will be able to tell you if you're unsure.

These extensions can be a few days or a couple of weeks, it's up to your Module Leaders, or person responsible for granting extensions, who will work within the university policy about what they are permitted to allow. An extension policy is something we have in place to prevent students from being impacted by emergencies or sudden life events (e.g. being rushed to hospital). We don't want to penalize students for something outside their control so we grant extensions so that students can navigate emergencies without additional stress. With the advent of emails being accessible through smartphones, it's easier than ever to send a quick message to your Module Leader and let them know what is happening. This is why it's so important to know everyone's email address, for those situations where life happens and you need some support.

Different universities have different regulations surrounding what can or can't be included in extensions, so be prepared to provide your reason for needing an extension, and you may or may not be required to provide evidence. Traditionally, computer-related issues are often not a reason for an extension (because we expect you to back up your work and there are usually thousands of computers on your campus that you have, often, 24-hour access to), however as more learning takes place online, and there is a greater variety of courses mixing digital with face-to-face teaching, this is starting to change. If you are not sure, ask your tutors and Module Leaders.

Extenuating Circumstances (Mitigation): When Things Go Wrong

> They can only help if you tell them the problem . . . you'll feel better after talking to people.
>
> **Kathy**

Sometimes life happens, and you get overwhelmed, are unable to complete work, and generally feel like things are going very wrong and you need support for your academic work. This could be because you get sick, someone you love gets sick, you have changed medication, you can't afford to get to university for a presentation, or any other myriad of reasons. Life doesn't stop while you're studying, and we recognize this. Particularly over the duration of the COVID-19 pandemic, we have seen a huge rise in applications for extenuating circumstances for illness and mental health issues. We don't want students dropping out because life got in the way, we want to support you through those difficult life circumstances so that you can complete your degree.

Sometimes, however, we can't help you manage your challenging circumstances with a simple extension (although we will definitely try this first if we can). But every university has a procedure where you can apply for your individual circumstances to be taken into account so that your grades aren't penalized by negative events in your life. Extenuating circumstances is where you apply to do the work later in the academic year.

It is important to remember that asking for, and being granted, extenuating circumstances does not get you out of doing the work; you are simply being allowed to postpone doing the work so that you can navigate your emergency without additional worry. You will have to complete the work eventually; it's more like a really big extension than anything else, except the work you are asked to do will look slightly different (e.g. a different essay title). You want to be sure that you really do need to apply for extenuating circumstances, since postponing completing the work might have a negative impact on other deadlines that are in the future, and there is also no guarantee your application will be accepted, thereby meaning you fail an assignment.

If you have your circumstances accepted as a reasonable excuse for not completing work then you will not incur a marking penalty when you come to do the work later in the academic year. Your university will have an official policy on this, there will be forms to complete and a specific email address that you need to send things to. You also need to tell your Programme Leader and/or Module Leader if you apply. Make sure you find out all this information now, just in case (see BOX 4.6). That way, if you need it, you're not worried about finding out who to speak to or how when things are already stressful.

BOX 4.6 Extenuating Circumstances Information

What my university calls Extenuating Circumstances/ Mitigation	
Where the policy is	
Where the form to apply is	
Where to send the form	
Who to send the form to	
Who to talk to on my course if I apply for Mitigation/ Extenuating Circumstances	
Personal Tutor	

What Happens if You Fail a Module (or Several. . .)

> You're your own person, you cannot blame [anyone else] for the mark that you got.
>
> Milo

Sometimes, for all sorts of reasons, you don't pass an assignment. This is often the first major point of panic for students. Many students have been used to a lot of additional help or have been out of education for a while, so have limited experience of actually failing an assignment. Even if you have, it's still a very stressful experience. However, there is a system in place to deal with this. The majority of universities will give you another opportunity to pass an assignment or exam, and this takes place in something called a 'resit' or 'referral' period (sometimes called a referral/deferral period).

The Referral/Resit Period

> *If you didn't do as well, it's not the end of the world. Go and speak to the lecturers, see where you went wrong.*
>
> **Alice**

We have something that's typically called a 'referral' or 'resit' period. This is where you get another chance to do your assignment. This might be within the term, or after the term has ended. This is not always broadcast on the university websites, usually because it is often different between programmes given their different requirements. But all your lecturers will know when it is for your university and degree programme, so just ask.

Things to remember for referral work:

1. You won't (normally) be able to do the same piece of work again. We can't allow you to answer the same question when feedback has already gone back to students, nor can we let you simply try again as this isn't fair on students who submitted and passed. So, we ask you to do an equivalent piece of work. This might be a different essay question, or it might be looking at a different data set. Whatever it is, it will have been checked by lots of people to be equivalent and fair.

2. Your work will probably be capped at 40%, the standard pass mark. In the majority of cases, we put a cap on the number of marks you can get. This is so that we can differentiate those students who passed first time and those who did not. However, most of the time we will let you know what your mark *would* have been, so always try your best and see how

well you can do. However, the exception to this is if you have mitigation/extenuating circumstances accepted, then we take this cap off your mark, and you get the awarded mark.

What is important to remember is that you shouldn't rely on the referral period to catch up, it is strictly there as an emergency for those students who don't/can't pass/submit first time. The referral period is also often outside term time, in your vacation time. If you do referrals you are giving up holiday to do them, so work hard during the year to avoid them if at all possible.

If things don't go to plan, typically you can have another opportunity to take and pass modules during the next academic year, but this means you are held back a year in your degree. There are financial implications for this, as well as the fact that you will no longer be learning with the friends you have made on the course, which is a big challenge for many students.

Sometimes, if you fail just the one module, you can 'trail' it into the next year. This means you study this module alongside the modules in your next year of study. And yes, that is what you're thinking, a lot more work. So, work hard during the year and get everything done if you can.

If you have to repeat a year of study, due to needing to repeat some modules, you may have the additional cost of fees and yet another student maintenance loan (see Chapter 3). So, unless there is a good reason for not completing your work, my advice is to ensure you get it done if at all possible. There are lots of ways we can support students who have unexpected challenges, health issues, or life difficulties to negotiate during their degree, and I'll cover those in Chapter 13. But we do understand that sometimes this is the best option for a student, particularly if their learning has been impacted by situations beyond their control. So, if you do have to repeat a year, look at it as a chance to learn more, to embed your knowledge so that in the following year, you can really aim high in your assignments.

A Final Word

> Plan well, listen carefully, stick to the questions asked on assignments, and ask for help if you need it. Enjoy this experience and be very proud you have made it this far.
>
> **Helen**

University is laid out in a pretty specific structure, and a lot of what I've written is probably feeling very alien right now, as well as a huge amount of information. Don't worry, most of this you will pick up really quickly when you get to university and during your first year of study. The regulations are there to guide you so that you know what you're doing; make sure to read them and the programme and module guides you're provided, so that you are clear how everything is going to work. Forewarned is always forearmed.

It is really important to remember that everything is about balance, including your studies. Yes, we have systems in place for when things go wrong, but it's helpful to ensure that you have good balance so that you're able to navigate these challenges without them impacting your degree too much. Just remember, know what you are doing and when, and know who to talk to if things go wrong; that way, if you get stuck, you know who to ask for help.

www.oup.com/he/parson1e

Visit the online resources where you will find additional materials including guides on time management, financial planning and budgeting, mindfulness and mental health, hints and tips, as well as all the tables from the book.

Chapter 5

THE FIRST WEEK
INDUCTION/FRESHERS' WEEK

Why This Chapter Is Important

- Freshers' Week is not just about having fun, it's an important transition point in your life before university and the next few years of study, this is why we now often now call it an 'induction' to university.
- The transition to university can be stressful for some students, so this chapter aims to equip you with what you need to know about this important transition period.

> Freshers' Week was important as it was my chance to step out of my comfort zone and do something different and get a feel for what to come.
>
> **Jamie**

All universities understand that coming to university is likely to be completely different from anything else you have experienced before; we know you will feel like a fish out of water for a while. That's why we have organized a whole variety of things for you to do when you get here, to help you feel a bit more comfortable with your new environment.

The first part of your university journey is called a transition period; with the help of something often called an 'Induction', we try and remove as many of the bumps in your transition to university as possible. The idea is to introduce you to how things work at university (generally), your department more specifically, and your fellow students—all to help you feel more comfortable in your new learning environment. We hope you will make friends, or at least begin to recognize enough of your fellow students to feel comfortable attending class. This transition period is particularly important for international and national students as you get the time to learn about the local area as well as meet the people you will be doing your course with, so that you can feel more at ease with your new place of study.

It used to be the case that we had a single week full of introductory activities for our students, to welcome them to university. We called this Freshers' Week, and there were societies inviting you to join them, nights out, and lots of talking from staff—and it was just new students who were on campus. This gave you a relatively gentle introduction to university and the campus/es before all the existing students arrived (of which there are usually thousands). Now it's morphed into something a little broader since student demographics have changed so much: it's certainly no longer a week-long party.

Many places still call it Freshers' Week (or Welcome Week), but that's just the week before term starts. Now, there's a whole lot more provided, some universities prefer the term 'Induction' (and other terms might also be used). One of the reasons we've changed the phrasing is that we don't always limit ourselves to a single week as we know that transition can sometimes take much longer than a week. Induction can now last several weeks, depending on the university you go to, and can sometimes start much earlier than the week before term starts. In addition, with the increase in blended learning courses and the use of virtual learning environments (VLEs) we now have a mix of online and offline induction activities for you to engage with that can help introduce you to how your new university works.

How this transition period is managed will vary between universities, sometimes quite a lot. So read your emails and keep hold of the timetable you've been given. If there is anything listed in this chapter that you're not aware of (e.g. your Personal Tutor), just ask one of the lecturers on your course and/or your Programme Leader.

A final note for this introductory section: many universities offer low-sensory or disability-friendly options for induction activities, so if you have particular support needs, make sure you let the university know ahead of starting. This should mean that any support you require can be put in place for you, enabling you to take part in this important transition period.

Making Notes and Remembering the Information You're Given

[The induction period] gradually pushes you in, so that when you do start lectures, you've already stepped up, so then you can start to go further.

Kathy

During induction, we throw a huge amount of information at you about how everything works on your course and in your university;

it will feel like a tidal wave of information washing over your head and may feel overwhelming at points. We understand this, so you'll get plenty of handouts (paper and/or digital) and emails, so that you can look at it all later when your head has stopped spinning a little! It's a good idea to set up a filing system at this stage (either digital or physical) so you can easily locate key information on a particular topic at a later date.

The biggest reason for the induction period is to meet people and get comfortable; if that happens then it's a great start, the information will be there waiting for you when you need it. For now, here's a quick checklist in BOX 5.1 for you to fill out later.

In this introductory period at university there will be inductions for your Virtual Learning Environment (VLE), introductions to Support

BOX 5.1 Checklist of Things to do in Freshers' Week

I have seen the library	
I have checked my student card works	
I know where the help desk is	
I have found the cafes, canteens, and coffee shops	
I know where the Students' Union is	
I know where Support Services are based	
I know how to get on to the VLE	
I know where my course information is	
I have found my modules on the VLE	
I know how to contact staff	
I know where my class timetable is	

Teams, Library tours, talks from the Students' Union, Programme talks, meetings with staff, and often plenty of hands-on activities to get you talking to each other. And yes, sometimes we even use those cringeworthy ice-breaker games—mostly because they make most students laugh and talk to each other without any pressure on those who aren't quite up for talking just yet.

You will get a lot of information in the induction period, and we know that many (most) students often forget it by the end of the week. Make as many notes as you can, but if you forget, don't worry. We make sure that you still have access to all this information after Induction (it will be in a space on your VLE and/or the university website itself). Your job is to make sure you know where it is, and to hang on to any bits of paper you are given. If you're not sure after Induction, it is still very much OK to ask for help.

Everyone Is Nervous

> [Freshers' Week is] crucial, I made friends and had enough time to settle in before actual learning started which took off a lot of pressure.
>
> **Mia**

It's completely normal to feel nervous around Induction and Freshers' Week; almost everyone feels nervous (even staff sometimes!). What you need to remember is that most people are feeling like this, whether they are local students, national students, or international students. So, the best thing you can do is to dive right in, talk to the person next to you, and go to as many of the events that have been laid on for you as you can. Go to your Student Union and ask about Student Societies that interest you, take part in local walks, events, and definitely go along to all the programme-related activities and talks. If you're an international student, try to arrive at your university as early as visas and finances allow, so that you can spend more time getting used to the campus and the city you will be living in for the duration of your UK university journey.

For some students this will be more challenging, and we are well aware that some students have more robust barriers to overcome such as social anxiety or fears over language barriers, which can prevent them taking part. If this applies to you, do your best to join in, you might find other students help you, but crucially, don't worry. All staff are available on email, and if you prefer to introduce yourself this way, then that is fine. Nobody is going to push you to do anything you're not comfortable with. Do your best to communicate, and you will find if you keep trying it is a skill that will develop naturally throughout your course.

You'll find that there are a variety of formal events for you to engage with, whether that is in person, or digitally. Some come from the University, and these are often the formal, 'vital' elements that you absolutely need for your studies. These comprise things like digital training, an overview of how your degree will work, and sometimes a welcome from the Vice-Chancellor themselves (they are the person who is in overall charge of the university).

Then you have events laid on by your department, which are all about meeting the staff who will teach you and meeting your fellow students. These should all be in accessible spaces so that students with all accessibility needs can access them. If you find you can't access something, contact your Programme Leader (or Course Leader) and let them know. Sometimes the things we put on are big talks, with all the new students in one room (all lecture rooms/halls should be completely accessible). Just remember that while big lecture theatres can feel very intimidating (they can be VERY big), almost everyone feels as nervous as you do, and the staff are doing their best to make you feel comfortable.

Your lecturers might also have some small-group activities, which are all focused around getting you talking to each other and understanding some of the ways in which your subject works. For example, in Psychology, we often have some fun experiments for people to get involved with so that new students can see psychology in action. I often have ice-breakers, and one of my favourites is 'Human Bingo', which gives students a gentle/neutral way of talking to each other without asking them to think about what to talk about.

You might even have specific, sometimes socially oriented, events targeted at certain demographics of students, such as mature students, international students, or care-experienced students. These events are particularly useful for students who might need additional support during their studies. You will meet new people at every event, along with finding a potential support network and lots of useful information.

There will often be student helpers around campus because we know that we (your lecturers) can sometimes seem a little intimidating at first for some students. Fellow students and peers can often be much more approachable for you, which is why we often ask student volunteers to help out in Freshers' Week itself. They will be showing you where to go, answering questions, taking you on tours of campus, generally helping you get used to your new space. They frequently work with the Students' Union for the week, so wear brightly coloured hoodies or T-shirts, and they are there to help share what they know, as well as help you if you get lost.

Joining In with Activities and Socializing

> It felt uncomfortable . . . and then [the lecturer] started making jokes and being smiley . . . it made me feel so much better . . . I didn't feel quite so intimidated.
>
> **Sarah**

As we've covered already, there will be a wide variety of things to do during induction and it's worthwhile engaging with them just so you get to know people on your course and the people who will be teaching you. Not everything will be something you want to do; not everyone wants to go clubbing, and equally not everyone wants to join a chess club. Have a look and join in with some of it, even if that's just the bits where you meet the staff and students on your course.

Nowadays we send through a timetable for the induction part of Freshers' Week, and the Students' Union (see below) will often send a list of events as well. Not everything scheduled in will be suitable for you but there are usually events for everyone, regardless of age group or home situation.

You can also find out lots of information about what is going on via the university websites. There is often a special splash page (the first page you see on the university website) directly targeted at new students around the start of term and this will have lots of links that will direct you to the different sections of Freshers' Week and the university systems you need.

All of the things we put together for new students are designed to help you get comfortable on campus, in the local area, and with each other, and help you get to know staff. If you start term a little bit more relaxed, you're going to take in a whole lot more in Week One, when all the important module information appears (i.e. what you'll be learning and information about how assessment will work).

While it can sometimes feel that social events revolve around alcohol for some areas of induction/Freshers' Week, it's important to remember that not everyone drinks alcohol, and there should never be any pressure on anyone to do so. Everyone is autonomous and should be given the respect and dignity to make their own choices. But remember, if you are the friend who isn't drinking (as I usually was), be extra vigilant and help keep your new friends safe while you're all having fun.

Meeting New People

> *Making friends is easy, I suffer from anxiety and this was my main concern, I thought to myself what a shame it would be to not make friends, so I plucked up the courage and started talking and made a bunch of friends.*
>
> **Jamie**

You are going to meet so many new people, from all walks of life and background, when you get to university: fellow students, academic staff, support staff, library staff, catering staff, porters, IT technicians, and everyone else who keeps a university running. This is one of the best things about attending university. Most of the people you will interact with are your lecturers and tutors (the academic staff), your fellow students, and support staff. It's really important to start talking to people as early as you can—that way you can start to feel more comfortable when it comes to asking questions later on. While it can be stressful to communicate with people you don't know, it is important that you are able to do so, or you won't be able to get the support you potentially need. There's a list of key contacts in BOX 5.2; fill that in so that you know where to find this information when you need it.

You may be allocated a Personal Tutor before you arrive on campus. Mental health among a student population is a big concern for universities, so we ensure that student support is available as early as possible and throughout your studies. Your Personal Tutor is someone I've added to most of the 'who to contact when you need support' lists throughout this book. They are the person who is there to support you on your academic journey, but they are not just there to talk about how well you are doing (or not) in your studies. Your Personal Tutor is a source of support and should be your first point of contact for anything in your life that is impacting your journey through university.

At university we know that life events can impact study, so we put in place tutors to ensure you have someone to notify and talk to about this. Personal Tutors are not always counsellors, but we will always know where you need to go to get support; we are able to signpost you

BOX 5.2 Key People

Person	Location	Contact details
The key person to speak to on my programme is:		
My Personal Tutor is:		
A lecturer I feel I can talk to is called:		
Another new student I feel I can talk to is:		
The Student Support Team		

to where you need to go if we can't help ourselves. Some universities have a dedicated team of Personal Tutors, and some allocate Personal Tutor roles to lecturers and tutors on your course. Make a note of your Personal Tutor and ensure you say hello to them in Induction Week.

For those of you with particular support needs, while we always recommend notifying the university ahead of time, Freshers' Week/ induction is the time to find the relevant support service and ensure that you have the necessary support in place for your studies. If you haven't already notified the university of support needs you have, then find the support services and make an appointment. Do not assume any support you had prior to university will be in place— universities are not told anything by colleges and other educational institutions, so it is up to you to let us know if you need support of any kind.

The other students on your course are now your peers; they are the people who you will spend a lot of time with for the next few years. It will always help to know other people on your course, but not everyone has equal levels of confidence when it comes to talking to new people. Talking to your fellow students is incredibly important, and nerve-wracking as it can be, I'm going to give you the same advice I gave my youngest brother many years ago—just dive in and say 'Hi' before you've had a chance to think about it too much. Honestly, most people will be so grateful if you say hello to them, because you'll find that almost everyone is just as nervous as you.

So, take a deep breath and say hello to the person you're sitting next to, ask their name and where they're from. You might not end up spending much time with the people you hang out with in Freshers' Week after you start classes, but you also might end up with friends for life. Some of my closest friends now are people I connected with in Freshers' Week.

The Students' Union

> *Freshers' Week gave me a chance to familiarize myself with the campus and facilities and read up on all the information about my course which was handed out. I found it useful talking to other students already studying my degree course.*
>
> **Mohammed**

Every university has something called a Students' Union, often made up of former and current students of the university. We have elections each year for student positions, and you'll find there are campaign leaflets and emails each year to ask you to vote for the next representative from the student community in the different positions. One day, you might even run for one of those positions yourself.

For now, in your induction period, you just need to know what they do. And that is a lot. Here's a list of things they are involved in:

1. Coordinating activities and student societies. These can be anything from sports clubs to debate clubs and chess clubs! There's something for everyone, often covering a wide range of beliefs, interests, and subjects. If there isn't one connected to a particular interest, belief, or subject, then you can ask about setting a club or society up yourself. Joining in with clubs and societies is great for developing new skills, developing language skills, and meeting new people, in particular for international students. You can get involved and learn new things, as well as meet people, alongside your degree, that will help you when you graduate.

2. Student support. They can direct you to where you need to go for support, and they can also lobby on your behalf for bigger issues impacting your mental health or well-being (i.e. if there is an issue in your halls of residence or on your course).

3. Social networking. There will be lots of social events organized by the Students' Union, and if there isn't anything you like the look of, just talk to them and ask if they'd think about putting something on. The variety is wide: I've seen walking tours, inflatable obstacle courses (which look so much fun!), even in-house karaoke events alongside the regular clubs and pubs events.

4. Discounts! Your student card entitles you to many, many, discounts: welcome to not having to pay full price for a lot of things both inside and outside university for a while. You may find there are more discounts available through your particular Students' Union, which they will let you know about.

During your induction period, you'll find representatives from the Students' Union are everywhere, often in brightly coloured T-shirts or hoodies, handing out leaflets, putting on fun things to do, and putting on a programme of social events just for Freshers' Week to help everyone get to know each other. You will often see events where all societies have stalls/tables and you can walk around, have a chat, then maybe join those you're interested in.

Finally, there are the freebies, from pens or pizza, to free shots at the local club. My advice is to walk around everything if you can, see what is on offer, make sure you take all the leaflets handed to you, and definitely get there in time to get any free pizza if it's available.

Digital Inductions

I think without freshers [week], uni would have been so hard. It's so much support and information in a week and it makes you feel a lot more relaxed as you start to get to know the campus.

Alex

As universities increasingly shift towards hybrid/blended course delivery, digital inductions are likely to be offered by your institution. Now it's an expectation that you will engage with your class materials and produce assignments digitally. We provide huge numbers of on-campus computers for those who lack computer access for various reasons, so you will always have access to computers to complete your work. By the time your course starts you will probably have been directed to lots of training and important links for the digital aspects of your course—most notably the Virtual Learning Environment (VLE), where all your course materials will be. You absolutely *have* to do this, even if you're a whizz with computers. Yes, the systems are generally straightforward, but you still need to know how they work. If you're nervous about computers and new programs, don't worry, the induction videos and sessions are usually aimed at those who are unsure, and everyone is there to help. Get used to using the VLE now, because this is usually where you will get all your course information and submit some, if not all, of your assignments.

One of the things you need to definitely make sure you do is check your email is set up and working. Many students forget about this in the rush of getting to university and the wide social programme available in the first week. One thing to get into the habit of doing from the very start of your degree is checking your university email account daily. Email is how we, your lecturers and the wider university, communicate with you, and how you should communicate with us outside of classes,

BOX 5.3 Digital Induction

I've checked my university email works	
I have downloaded any apps that the university has (e.g. timetable/general/attendance)	
I have set my university email up on my phone (not everyone's preference, but very useful to do)	
I have done the digital induction to the VLE and know how to get to all my modules	
I know where the IT help resources are (online and offline)	

so checking it works is vital. If you have any problems, let a lecturer on your course know or, better yet, find the IT support desk/technicians. Induction is the time to find that out and make sure you have access ahead of your course starting. BOX 5.3 provides a checklist of what you need to make sure you've done during the first week at university.

Keeping Safe on Campus

While university is an amazing place to be and has an incredible atmosphere - it does not mean to say that you should forget safety procedures that you would usually follow.

Marshall

While university campuses are relatively safe spaces, it's always sensible to take basic precautions while you're at university. Here are some

Top Tips for staying safe while socializing. The chapter on socializing (see Chapter 11) has a lot of information for when you're out and about, including more detail on many of these Top Tips, so I recommend reading that as well before you go out.

—— VANESSA'S TOP TIPS ——
for staying safe while socializing

> *University is no different to a town you may not know—no different to walking home alone—treat it the same way as you would anywhere else.*
>
> **Kaylie**

- Keep your Student ID safe.
  - Ideally separate from your keys and on a lanyard around your neck.
- Get a waterproof (this is the UK!) bag/backpack with internal compartments for keys and purse/wallet.
- Keep your phone in your pocket or in your bag.
- If you have a bike, get a decent security lock.
- Make your social media account is private.
- Let friends know where you're going when you're out and about.
- Lock windows and doors when you leave your flat/house/halls.
- Keep your belongings with you.
  - Don't leave them lying around a café, class, or the library.
- Put the Security Services and Campus Police numbers into your phone.
- Make sure you are familiar with your campus!

- This is a top safety tip, if you know where you're going, you will walk with confidence and be able to get where you need to more quickly.

- Don't go out alone, and avoid walking alone at night.

- Don't feel pressured into doing anything you don't want to do.

- Learn local/national alert signals (e.g. Ask Angela).

- Stay vigilant, particularly if you're out at night.

- Make sure you know what to do if anything negative happens when you are out.

- If you see anything suspicious, report it to the relevant person.
  - See BOX 5.4.

BOX 5.4 provides a list of core services you can report safety-related issues to. There are spaces to add other services your university might have.

BOX 5.4 Security and Reporting

Service	Phone Number/ Contact Method
Campus Security Team	
Campus Police	
Student Advice Point	
University Web-based Reporting Service	
Personal Tutor	
Programme Leader	
Another Lecturer I know/trust	

A Final Word

> [Freshers' Week is] quite important because even though you might think you won't be learning much; it helps you gain a basic understanding of what you're working towards in your degree but also allows you to meet some of the people on your course. I met most of the friends I made at university during Freshers' Week and still keep in touch now after graduation.
>
> **Bethany**

The main thing to remember is to have fun, get to know a few people, and try to get your head around the digital stuff. It's all new, we know you're nervous and sometimes meeting new people can be stressful, but we're all here to welcome you and help you begin to feel comfortable in your new university world. If you get to Week 1 and know at least one other person and can recognize a couple of your lecturers, that's a pretty good start.

www.oup.com/he/parson1e

Visit the online resources where you will find additional materials including guides on time management, financial planning and budgeting, mindfulness and mental health, hints and tips, as well as all the tables from the book.

Chapter 6

STUDY

Why This Chapter Is Important

- Understanding how the components of your degree fit together and what is required of you in classes will help you navigate your learning experience.
- Knowing where to get specific support for academic study will help you overcome academic challenges during your time at university.

> One assignment at a time. Find your way of learning and be patient; as they say, 'Rome wasn't built in a day'.
>
> **Charlie**

During your studies you will take several modules, attend numerous classes, and complete many assignments. We covered the mechanics of how all of this fits together in Chapter 4. Now we need to look at how to access your classes, where to access the study skills help and support provided by the university, and how to get the most out of this educational experience. This chapter is invaluable in successfully navigating your degree and covers a significant amount of information, so it's all really important; read this chapter carefully. Forewarned is forearmed, and this chapter will give you a whole host of advice about what is expected of you in classes and in your studies, so that you can be well prepared for the university academic journey.

Accessing Your Classes

Go for it, but make sure your priorities are right. Attend every lecture and take notes!

Aisha

As we touched upon in Chapter 4, there are various degree formats available now, and what you experience will be bespoke to your university and course. All your classes may be held on campus, you might attend half your classes on campus, or you might attend all your classes online. The different types of learning formats have different names, and you will see those on university websites now. In Table 6.1. I've broken down the most common terms used and what they mean.

Even before the COVID-19 pandemic there were signs of an increase in online/distance learning/hybrid courses becoming available. Since the pandemic, due to the range of resources developed during the periods of online learning, there has been an acceleration in this trend

Table 6.1 Styles of Information Provision at University

Type of learning format	What it means
Face-to-Face (F2F), on campus	Your classes are on campus and you will see your lecturers and tutors in person.
Distance learning	Your learning takes place in the traditional distance format. Materials are provided and there may, or may not, be some in-person sessions to attend during your course.
Blended learning	There is a relatively stable mix of on-campus and online content delivery on your course.
Hybrid learning	There is a flexible mix of on-campus and online content delivery on your course, which is responsive to changes in situation. Here the focus is the on-campus classes, and online material is typically there to support those on-campus classes, but there may be online classes as well.

for flexibility, given the variety of technological options now available to staff in their teaching. This trend for flexible learning fits neatly with the changing student population, so it is likely these changes will continue, simply as they allow for greater variety and quality of teaching (which can only be a good thing).

It is important to remember that, with blended and hybrid learning in particular, there will be local variations within your particular programme, and the idea behind these programmes is to deliver the most varied and exciting course possible in as responsive a manner as possible that benefits all students. There are huge advantages to hybrid and blended learning courses as they enable more students to access university while juggling their family and working lives. Funnelling all materials through the VLE (virtual learning environment, see later in the chapter) means that materials and lecture recordings can be accessed at any time of day from any device connected to the internet, meaning students can prepare for on-campus classes at a time that suits them.

In addition, there are significant benefits to on-campus teaching as we have more scope to directly engage you in activities which can allow for greater skill development in on-campus classes. You will find some details of how your degree will be delivered on your university website, but if there are none, you can contact the programme teams to find out a bit more.

Your Classes: AKA Your Modules

You will be blown away with all the different modules and topics, and sometimes it may just blur into one big mess. Keep it organized and try to manage your workload as best as possible.

Alice

As we mentioned in Chapter 4, your degree consists of various different modules. It's important that you know the names of your modules and their codes; at the start it's important to write them down and make an effort to remember them. Apart from anything else, you need to know who to contact if you have questions. In BOX 6.1 you'll see where you can add your own modules: names, codes, and who is in charge of them.

Some of your modules are called CORE modules, and these are ones you *have* to take. Sometimes these are core modules because there are specific requirements from professional bodies such as the British Psychological Society (BPS, applies to all accredited Psychology courses) or the General Medical Council (GMC, applies to all degrees allied to medicine). But sometimes, these modules are core to

BOX 6.1 Modules and Module Leaders

Module Name	Module Code	Module Leader	Module Leader Email Address
e.g. Digital Humans	PSY385	Vanessa Parson	xxx.xxx@ universityname. ac.uk

all students to make sure you have all the foundational knowledge required for the subject you are studying.

Then there will be other modules called OPTION modules, sometimes called ELECTIVES. Most students will get to design part of the degree around what they are interested in, but the point at which you're able to choose optional modules will depend on your degree. Some programmes allow you to choose maybe one or two optional modules in the first year of study, while others only allow this from the second/third year. You'll get given a series of choices within your programme, but you may also be able to take modules outside your programme as well. Figure 6.1 shows some typical core and elective modules that might be found on a psychology degree. Each stage has a number of core modules that have to be taken, and each year there are options made available. There is always a lot of expected content coverage in the first two years of study, but will see that as you go through the programme the specificity of content increases, as does the expectation of detail (moving from 'Introduction to Research Methods' to 'Advanced Research Methods').

Figure 6.1 Example Module Structure

Stage 1/Level 4 (first year)

Core Modules
- Introduction to Psychology
- Introduction Research Methods in Psychology
- Introduction to Mental Health

Option Modules
- Current Issues in Psychology
- Option outside of Psychology

Stage 2/Level 5 (second year)

Core Modules
- Social and Developmental Psychology
- Biological and Cognitive Psychology
- Advanced Research Methods and Statistics

Option Modules
- Anomalous Psychology
- Neurodiversity
- Evolutionary Psychology in Practice
- Option outside of Psychology

Stage 3/Level 6 (third year)

Core Modules
- Critical Issues in Psychology
- Dissertation

Option Modules
- Cyberpsychology
- Advanced Perception
- Humour and Emotion
- Advanced Statistics
- Psychology in the Real World
- Mental Health and Illness
- Clinical Neuropsychology

As you move through your degree you will find you get more choice about what you study, so for many programmes (with some exceptions like Medicine), you get to choose a lot more options and ensure your degree covers the topics you really enjoy.

You might be able to elect to take a module outside of your programme if you don't want to take the available option on your programme; this is why option modules are sometimes called electives. You can sometimes 'elect' to take another subject as long as it fits in with your timetable and you get the permission of the programme leader. There are different rules around this though, and you might be restricted to certain subjects and in particular years, so it's wise to check with your programme leader if you have questions around option/elective modules. Obviously this is a specific example, but you get the idea.

When choosing modules my advice is to not get too hung up on your future plans. Yes, you should absolutely take the option modules that help you learn information you'll find useful later on. But don't ignore the ones that sound like fun but might not necessarily fit with your future career. University is one of the few times in your life that you'll get to study a whole range of things just because you find them interesting. At the end of the day, your final degree title and grade will be what employers see, not your list of modules. Learning can be exciting so by all means indulge in some of the fun modules; they're likely to bring you extra transferable skills, and may even give you something to think about when it comes to your future.

Another piece of advice I have about options is to not look at what your friends are taking when you decide. University can be an intimidating place, so hanging out with your friends all the time is very tempting, and it can be reassuring when you start a new course. But keep in mind that this is YOUR degree, so do what you are interested in; you will perform your best in your work when you are interested in what you study.

Ultimately, you won't spend your life working around your mates unless you're really lucky, so just do your thing, learn what you are interested in, and develop your independence. Then meet your friends between/after classes.

There are a few exceptions to this system of option modules, one of which is Medicine. You need to study a very specific set of materials to ensure that the requirements of the GMC are met and you graduate able to progress to the next phase of your studies. Sometimes, for this reason, all your modules on a course are CORE modules.

Making the Most of Classes

> *Turn up to class, engage in lessons, you're only going to get out what you put in.*
>
> **Anthony**

You will have different types of classes during your studies: lectures, workshops, seminars, practical classes, and there may be other names used as well. Lectures involve delivery of core material; you'll be expected to listen and take notes. All your other classes are usually more practical, involving activities, discussions, and engaging with specific materials to create a specific outcome. Online learning is much the same: digital lectures are for listening to and taking notes, the rest of the materials and contact sessions are for more practical engagement with the material you need to learn.

Taking notes is vital, it's a key part of every single class you go to. I am eternally confused by students who show up to class without so much as a pen and notepad, because there is no way to remember everything you did in every class, or contribute to anything class-related unless you have some kind of note-taking option (computer/notepad, whatever works for you). Even Einstein wrote notes: take the hint.

VANESSA'S TOP TIPS
for making the most of your classes

> Print your seminar worksheets and lecture slides out in notes format. It'll save you so much time and you'll be able to write down the useful things you're taught, rather than the basic facts which are already written out.
>
> **Sarah**

When it comes to making the most out of your classes and studies, the best advice is always:

- Turn up
- Listen
- Take part
- Write notes
- Do the reading

Taking Part in Your Classes

> I never wrote down what was on the slide, I wrote down what the lecturer said that wasn't on the slide.
>
> **Milo**

Engaging in a class is often the most challenging aspect for some students, particularly if you're anxious about talking to people you don't know, or English isn't your first language. What you need to remember, as I mention in Chapter 5, is that almost everyone is nervous. Lots of people will be anxious, and this is perfectly normal for the majority of students. So, take a deep breath and start talking. (Although maybe not if the lecturer is talking!)

However, some students do get rather more anxious talking in front of others, particularly people they don't know. So, if this is something you recognize in yourself, don't worry. You are in class and that's great, you're listening and engaging just by being present and responding in a non-verbal manner. Remember, you can always send questions to your tutor via email or a university messaging system (any system that can send a digital message, e.g. Microsoft Teams™) after class. You will adjust to your new peer group, but this does not happen at the same speed for everyone. Be patient with yourself and others while you become accustomed to the group of people you will spend the next few years learning alongside.

Sometimes you might find it easier to interact with your peers and lecturers via the computer, at least initially. If this is the case for you, that's absolutely fine. Make the most of this so that in face-to-face teaching, you have a bit more confidence interacting and/or don't feel nervous or anxious about being quiet.

If your seminars are running online, make sure you turn your camera on and communicate through chat (or microphone if you can). There are few things more challenging from a teaching perspective than an online class where nobody has their camera on and nobody wants to communicate! You will place yourself at a disadvantage if you don't interact, and remember, if you're worried about being in an online class while still wearing pyjamas, chances are that your tutor is also wearing pyjama bottoms if they're working from home! We're not worried about what you're wearing; the most important thing is that you're there and engaging with the class.

Seminars do involve discussions, interactive activities, and putting information together, for the most part. Academics can get quite creative with how they teach, so there are lots of different things involved in seminars now. Some seminars will require you to read material in advance, and they frequently require you to have been to (or watched) the previous lecture. Make sure you do the reading before you do, otherwise you *will* struggle.

Workshops and practical classes involve more hands-on work, such as learning statistics or engaging in experiments or physical activities. With these, you need to be prepared to be involved and, more often than not, work in groups of people, some of whom you might not know very well. Just remember, most of your fellow students are new, and you'll soon find people you're comfortable working with.

It's worth bearing in the mind the reasons why seminars and workshops are interactive and/or practical in their approach, and one of the main reasons is related to employability. Being able to interact with a range of people, to question, to engage in teamwork, or to run experiments help you develop skills that are required and valued in the workplace. Seminars provide you with a wonderful opportunity to build on your communication skills and gain confidence in speaking with all different kinds of people, for example. Plus, being able to actively listen and question (in a constructive manner) is evidence of critical thinking, which is a key skill that employers are increasingly on the lookout for.

To ensure that the classroom is a comfortable place for everyone, try to be a positive presence in class. Allow others the space to explore their own learning without fear of negative feedback, and try to avoid taking over discussions. Some people may take longer than others to communicate their points—give them the space they need to do so without interrupting, and where appropriate offer supportive comments or demonstrate positive body language (e.g. selective nods). A classroom situation should be a safe space for everyone to develop their learning and explore ideas, so try not to judge your fellow students. When students unintentionally take over discussions (sometimes with personal anecdotes which have no place in a classroom situation) and voice negative opinions that affect others, it can lead to a very unconformable learning situation.

VANESSA'S TOP TIPS

for engaging with class

> You get back what you put in
> **Nikolas**

A quick word on classroom etiquette. Here are a list of DOs and DON'Ts for when you're in your classes (all classes):

- **Do** show up on time.
  - We've got a set amount of material to get through; if you're late, you've missed stuff, and you may disrupt the rest of the class.

- **Don't** talk unless asked.
  - Unless you are invited to ask questions or discuss material, you should be quiet in classes. It's distracting for lecturers to hear constant whispering while we're talking, and your fellow students are all trying to work. If you don't want to listen, that's up to you, but don't distract us or the rest of the class. Besides, if you're talking, you're not listening and you'll miss what we say!

- **Do** write notes.
  - Computer or paper, it's your preference, just make sure you take notes.

- **Don't** text your friends.
  - (We absolutely know what is happening when students are looking down and giggling into their laps. . .!)

- **Don't** play games or watch shows on your phone/computer.
  - It distracts other people and we very much notice what you're doing.

- **Do** try to stay awake.
  - (And if you do fall asleep please don't snore or drool. . .!)

Be respectful of others, be inclusive, and ensure that you aren't the reason someone else doesn't like the class they're in.

Make sure that if there are any issues with the group you're working with, you try and sort it out yourselves as this is practising vital negotiation and group management skills. Ideally you will do this between yourselves, but the lecturers and tutors are all there to help support you during class; we will intervene and support you if there are any significant issues.

Just remember that having a support plan/memo in place does not mean you can skip communication in class. Classrooms are safe spaces for you to develop your skills, and that absolutely involves respectful verbal communication. Unless you're planning on living as a hermit in the Outer Hebrides, your work life will involve speaking to, and working with, people, so start learning this skill as soon as you can.

The Many Uses of a Library

Use the library as much as possible, the people who work there know what they are talking about and are really helpful.

Anthony

Your library at university is likely to be huge, over several floors (and sometimes several buildings), and with a complicated coding system to help you to find what you're looking for. Resources related to your subject will probably be in a particular section, but they might also be spread over several sections and/or floors. Then you have access to paper copies of journals (often historical, most access is online for journals now), and these journals fill yet another floor or building. Some universities have departmental libraries where all the books and journals considered part of your academic subject are located. This doesn't mean you will never need books or journals outside of this though, so make sure you know where all books and journals are stored. Your best bet at finding any books is through the library website on the university internal website.

It's not just physical books/articles that you find in libraries now, there are eBooks, journal articles, newspapers, magazines, and all sorts of software and resources available. And there's more still within the libraries themselves. Your university library will contain numerous computers you can use for free (often 24 hours a day) and is staffed by librarians and assistants who can help you find items and answer questions. Sometimes you will find support staff who can help you with study skills questions, running training and drop-in study support sessions, etc. The list goes on: the library is a really important hub of activity all designed around supporting you in your studies.

The library website gives you access to not only lists of physical books but also all the eBooks and additional resources the university can share. You will find information about some of the additional support and activities they provide, both on campus and online. But the most effective way to find out everything your library has to offer is to go and look around, work out where the main section for books on your course is and have a look at what is available. You should also take (or download/bookmark) a copy of every leaflet they have; these will have contact details and session times for drop-in sessions.

You will find a lot of university libraries have Study Skills Support sessions organized; some universities run Study Skills Support from other departments, but the library will always have details of these. Wherever the support for study skills is within your particular university, make a note of when they run, whether they are on campus or online, or where you can find out. These are run by experienced staff, they are for all students, and they are designed to help you with your academic skills, primarily writing and referencing. Look at the website and the leaflets they have available, and make a note of which sessions they run in BOX 6.2. below. Then, make sure you go along and get support.

Most libraries have social media accounts now, and most universities and individual departments and programmes use Twitter and Instagram in particular. You're likely to see the many social media handles listed on public-facing websites and marketing materials. If you have social media accounts you should follow the library as a priority (as well as the university, Students' Union, and your own programme of course).

One thing you do need to remember though is that a library has a lot of people in, all the time, so treat it like a public space. If you're studying in the library and you've brought your laptop and phone with you, don't wander off to get a coffee or go to the bathroom; never leave your personal belongings unattended.

BOX 6.2 Study Skills Sessions

Study Skills Sessions Your University Puts on for Students	Times, Dates, Places

Negotiating Technology

> *Organization's key . . . the world is going digital [but] don't be scared to get a pen and paper out and write it down.*
>
> **Milo**

Much of your university work will be provided online, whether you are doing an online degree, blended/hybrid learning degree, or a fully face-to-face degree. While some of these digital changes have come about due to the lockdowns during the COVID-19 pandemic, this is actually to save resources and to allow more students to access university, and in fact, universities have been using some of these resources for many years. We will give you all the materials from classes in digital format—it allows us to provide handouts prior to classes, give you recordings of your lectures to listen to later on (which are really beneficial when it comes to revision), and effectively provide all the information you need during your time at university in one central, easy-to-access digital site.

VLEs (Virtual Learning Environments, e.g. Blackboard™ or Canvas™) are what we use to share your course information and resources with you, and these have a wide range of functionality, which means we can provide a good variety of resources to help you with your studies, such as module guides, print-out timetables, lecture slides and recordings, lists of questions, suggested references, useful YouTube videos (e.g. TED Talks), all broken down by module and class topic. They can often also support a lot of digital activities, such as webinars and live chats. We work really hard on these module spaces, and they are particularly important for anyone doing a blended/hybrid learning or online degree. You should learn your way around your modules and the VLE early on so that you don't miss out on your course materials and information.

Some VLEs now have an accompanying app (e.g. Canvas™), which can be incredibly useful, particularly if you're juggling a family and a job. However, make sure you don't rely on the app to produce work though. Smartphones are great, but they're too small to do any real work on them, and there is always more functionality available via the computer itself (see Chapter 3, 'Technology and your Course', for more information on purchasing/acquiring a suitable computer for your studies).

There are also the additional digital resources you will find provided. Some universities use Microsoft Teams™, all use email, and there are many other digital programs and apps in use across the UK. It's important to become familiar with all the digital expectations on your course, so that you can effectively take part in all learning opportunities on your course. This includes software you are expected to use (e.g. Open Sesame and SPSS or JASP). Embrace the fact that life at university is highly digital now, get suitable equipment, learn the skills, and ensure that you are fully able to participate in, and complete, your course.

It's important to remember that it's now a legal requirement in the UK for universities to ensure digital sites and materials are accessible and inclusive for all students, so you should see this within the materials provided to you. If you have any questions about this, you should contact your Module Leaders.

Using Computers

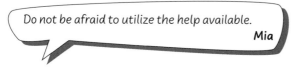

Do not be afraid to utilize the help available.

Mia

With an increasing move towards blended/hybrid learning, your computer skills are going to be developed whether you're expecting that or not. Most of your assignments, if they're written, will be constructed in word-processing packages, and you'll be expected to learn how to use various pieces of software you might not have encountered before. For example, you'll learn how to use various statistics packages (e.g. SPSS, JASP, or R) if you're studying any of the Social Sciences or Sports, and you might even get a chance to create your own programmes, such as in Psychology, using software such as Open Sesame, PsychoPy etc.

If you're not very confident using computers, don't worry, there are plenty of resources available to help you, and there is always an IT help system in place. You'll probably find you're better than you think, but until you get confident, just remember to watch the tutorials and take your time. Plan ahead if you're nervous of technology; that way you won't be nervous when you're completing assignments, enabling you to focus on what you're writing.

How Not to Write Assignments on Your Phone!

> Smartphones don't always give you everything, you need to use your laptop or library computer if you struggle.
>
> **Charlie**

What we've noticed over the last few years is students writing assignments on their phones. I know smartphones are fully kitted up with software these days, but typing with your thumbs isn't writing, and the screen is far too small for you to get a sense of what you're writing or the argument you're putting together. As assignment is a complete piece of work, not just a series of sentences.

What we are also aware of is that not all students have computers, so this is one reason they *do* write assignments on their phones. At university we have huge numbers of computers that are all free to use for our students. They are all up to date with the latest software, have full access to our library, the VLE, and any databases you need for your assignments, and they are often available 24/7, complete with security staff to make sure you're safe. Even for those doing blended/hybrid learning degrees, the on-campus computers are always available to you if you don't have access to one at home.

Not all students can come into university every day, so the way to take advantage of these computers is to work between classes and not just sit in the cafés chatting. It's really tempting to go to the café between classes and hang out with friends, and sometimes you should absolutely do this. But make sure that most days you knuckle down and make use of the resources we provide. When you're not around computers, you can use good old-fashioned pen and paper, and there's still very little in the digital world that beats this when it comes to retaining and learning the information. Get organized and plan your time; that way you won't be stuck around assignment submission time.

Netiquette: Communicating with Staff Online

Remember you are at university, and not sending a text!

Mrs E

You'll send and receive a significant number of emails and messages at university, and more specifically, you'll be communicating with your lecturers on a very regular basis, so it's important to remember some basic rules when it comes to this digital communication.

Let's start with emails. You're likely to be really familiar with most messaging services (any digital system or service that can send a message, e.g. WhatsApp™), but emails are different; they're a digital letter. Sounds obvious, but students often make mistakes in emails when contacting lecturers such as not including their name, any form of greeting, being over-familiar, adding an 'x' on the end of their name, or sometimes without any details at all which means we aren't able to answer the questions being asked.

══════════ VANESSA'S TOP TIPS ══════════

for emailing your lecturers

> *Every email you receive as part of your course is important. Take time to read them and reply promptly when asked.*
>
> **Jon**

Here's a list of some essential information to include when you communicate with staff:

- Basic greeting—e.g. 'Hello', or 'Dear Vanessa', or 'Dear Dr Parson' (or however your lecturers prefer being referenced).
  - A quick point to note here. I often get called Mrs Vanessa or Mrs Parson, which is incorrect, but is typically due to a very respectful translation error from international students. It is important to remember that most academic staff have Dr or Professor as their official title: this is what is accurate and respectful, so please use that. If you are unsure, either try searching for previous correspondence from that lecturer or locate their academic profile page on the university website which will usually list their title.
  - If your lecturer replies to your initial email using only their first name in their email signature, that usually gives you the 'green light' to address them using their first name in the rest of the email exchange.
- Include your name.
  - You can usually set up an automatic signature on your emails, where you can put your name, your course, and your student identification number—all the things we need in order to respond directly.
- State which module/assignment your email is about (if you wish to talk about a module/assignment).
  - And which programme you're on (which course you're doing)

- Add a sensible subject line, e.g. 'Question about Essay for Introduction to Psychology'.

- Be clear what your question/message is.

- Finish with a sensible and polite sign off with your preferred name, e.g. 'Best wishes'.

When emailing a lecturer ensure that your langauge and tone is appropriate. Make sure you never write emails like you're writing to your friends over chat/text/messaging/social media. Introduce yourself, give details about your question (e.g. year group, module, assignment, issue), and give us something to work with so we can help. Without some basic details we'll just reply and ask for them, and that may delay you getting the help you need.

You might also communicate with us (and we with you) via the VLE on discussion boards or using collaborative messaging packages such as Microsoft Teams™, and even sometimes on social media groups created for your course. Within this format you will find that communication becomes a little less formal and more relaxed. You can absolutely dispense with all the formalities of an email using these communication tools; just remember to stay reasonably professional.

It's also useful for you to remember that we get a lot of emails and communication each day, and while we want to reply as quickly as we can, sometimes we're busy (and none of us is expected to reply to emails over the weekends). Most universities have a time policy relating to replies to emails, but most teaching staff try to reply much more quickly than that. Just be patient, and once you've waited the length of the university policy (e.g. 72 hours/3 days) then it's OK to email again politely.

The most important thing to remember about emails is to check them regularly. You should check your university email account *and* any university messaging services (e.g. Microsoft Teams™) at least once a day; that way you won't miss anything.

How to Get Help with Writing Skills

> [There is] no shame in accepting help. No-one will judge you.
> **Mohammed**

Not everyone does well in their writing straight away; we know that you will all improve your writing skills as you go through your degree, but sometimes you need some support early on. So, if a tutor says you need to work on your writing, don't panic—just pay attention to the feedback you've been given and work on it.

We have a whole host of resources available for you, as well as support sessions (see BOX 6.2), through the library, study skills teams, disability support services, your academics and course materials, extra materials available online, and of course lots of book-based writing and study skills resources that you can use. There are numerous study skills and academic writing/communication books available, and finding one related to your subject will be really helpful. There are resources and avenues for support for everyone who needs them, and you will find the support to develop strategies that work for you, enabling you to improve your skills during your degree. This suite of support is particularly important to access if you have dyslexia or any other neurological/physical difference that means you will need extra help around the production of your academic work.

Academic writing is something that most students worry about, at least to some degree, but there isn't any need to worry. We want you to write in a particular way at university; often fairly formally, clearly, and with good spelling, punctuation, grammar, and structure.

These things are important for communicating clearly, however what many of you learned in school is not quite what we're after. If you can't remember what a fronted adverbial is, don't worry about it, I'd have to look it up too. What we care about is that you can clearly communicate what you understand. You can already do this to an extent, or you wouldn't be at university.

What you need to remember is that writing is all about communication—you need to show that you can share what you understand in relation to the questions we ask you. The biggest difference at university is that we want you to write a little more formally than you might be used to, and you won't get away with copying information from Google. Remember, practice makes perfect. If you're not sure you're writing well enough, do more writing, and ask for feedback! It's always the best way. You might want to do extra essays, or start a blog, write articles or stories. All writing is good practice, the more you write, and the more you apply the feedback you get from that writing, the better you will get.

If you struggle with academic writing, your lecturers and the resources provided throughout the university are your first ports of call. There are plenty of sources of support, and they'll be available throughout your time at university.

How Not to Screw up Your Assignments!

> Write an assignment plan, do more than one draft, and try not to rush any assignments. If you are struggling with the content, speak to your lecturers.
>
> **Kai**

The first obvious thing to say is don't leave them until the last minute! So many students do this, then they run out of time and get stressed.

We don't want this; all assignment deadlines are carefully planned so you have enough time—if you start when we tell you to. You need to plan your year, there are lots of assignments to do, and you need to fit them around all your other commitments. Plan ahead, and stay on top of things. You should already have written down your list of assignments in Chapter 4 (see BOX 4.6); don't forget to keep adding to this, and make sure you add all your deadlines into your calendar/s (phone, wall calendar, diary, etc.).

Start writing early. I cannot stress this enough. Leave yourself enough time to write drafts and do the reading. You need to do both to be successful. If you're not used to writing a draft of your work and editing it (proofreading, checking for sense, structure, and checking citations, etc.) to produce the final thing, then you're about to be!

Make sure you read the assignment brief carefully early on, that way you have a chance to ask questions if you don't understand what is being asked of you. Make sure you get to every class that's directly related to the assignment, or catch up later: make sure you don't miss any instructions. If you have questions, ask the Module Leader and/or lecturer/tutor who teaches you on the module for that particular assignment in plenty of time; don't leave your questions until the day of the deadline! Don't ask another member of staff, they won't be able to help; always go straight to the person in charge of that module or the person teaching you in class.

It's often been said that the best way to find mistakes is to click submit, but you really can avoid this if you leave enough time to plan to have a short break between writing and proofreading. Give yourself 24 hours before you start editing/proofreading your work. That way you won't read what you think is there; you'll read what is actually there, and you'll see all the typos and mistakes that you need to fix. You can also consider asking a trusted family member, or a friend/housemate on a different course to read through it as they will be able to spot paragraphs that don't make sense or find stray typos. Just make sure you don't email your work to anyone, or ask anyone to email their work to you; even if you're trying to help it's not worth the risk (see the section on Academic Misconduct below).

Many students try to sound impressive when they write assignments, so they consult a thesaurus to find other 'bigger and better' words to say the same thing. Take it from me, it doesn't work. What it shows is that you don't have the confidence to communicate clearly and you're trying to sound like a journal article. There's a balance to be struck where formality is concerned; yes, university-level writing will likely be more formal than the writing you have done previously, but you should avoid artificially inserting complex terminology in order to give the impression you are 'clever'. It's worth remembering that not all journal articles are written clearly, and the best-written ones are those that are easy to understand.

The key to a good assignment is clarity of communication. You don't need a lot of long words for people to think you're clever. We can see if you've understood the assignment by the information you have used and how clearly you can explain it. If you want your writing to improve, read more and write more, it really is that simple. The more journal articles and textbooks you read, the more your vocabulary will expand and the better your writing will get. Your confidence in communicating will improve too.

Feedback: Aims, Misconceptions, and What to Do with It

> *Read the feedback and use it to help you plan your next assignment; it's not criticism, it is there to help and guide you.*
>
> *Emma*

When we mark your work, we (usually) give you lots of feedback. This can be in many formats: verbal, general written comments, specific written comments in the text, or lists of criteria with selected sections for where you scored. There are many ways to give feedback, and your course and university will have specific ways of doing this. It's the written and verbal feedback that is the most use for you, because that will often give you specific pointers about what went wrong and what you can improve.

Sometimes it is difficult to accept constructive feedback; it can feel like we are being criticized personally, and not always just in an academic sense. It's important to remember that your academic feedback is framed as supportively as possible; we want to help you improve your work and that's why we put a lot of effort into writing down and sharing how you can do better. Your feedback is a reflection on your work, it is never a reflection on you. So, try to put your personal views to one side about how well you *think* you have done, and really listen to what we say about how well you have *actually* done. Remember, you are learning from the experts, so respect that they know more than you and are able to give you advice about how to improve your work. Nobody gets it perfectly right the first time, but there are always ways to improve, no matter how experienced you are.

The main thing you need to do is read the feedback carefully, ask if you aren't quite sure what it means, and then act on it in your next assignments. And I don't just mean the assignments that look exactly the same as that one. **ALL assignment feedback relates to ALL assignments**. Read, think, learn. That's how it all works.

Let's look at an example; we'll use an example of something that is often misunderstood—critical analysis. Imagine you have received a marked essay back from a lecturer and some of the comments in the feedback are 'Lacks depth' or 'Try to critically analyse the content in relation to the question more clearly'.

It's not always clear precisely what you need to do, so in response to this feedback, you could:

- Ask your lecturer for clarification if you're not sure what they mean.

- Critical analysis is a skill most students need to improve so have a look at the resources already available to you at your university.
  - Study guides which include sections on critical thinking (which you are likely to be able to access physically or remotely through the library).
  - Visit the study skills department/staff at your university to ask them what support they could offer.

- There are likely to be helpful YouTube™ videos by academics and authors available to support your writing development.

Academic Misconduct: Assignment Shortcuts that Break the Rules

The most important thing is reading, widely. You'll see that there is good and bad writing published. The good stuff is clear and succinct, and doesn't look like the author swallowed a thesaurus.

Faye

Hopefully you will know by now that it's not a good idea to just copy and paste work from the internet into assignments. But educational systems pre-university often don't penalize students who 'Google™' instead of think, so many students are used to writing essays like that, and it's something that often gets picked up suddenly in university.

All the information that you read in books, journal articles, prior essays from previous students, and anything on the internet has been written by someone else. This means it is covered by copyright and is the work of someone else. All of which means that if you copy it and pass it off as your own then you're going to get into trouble, because that is called intellectual theft. This includes buying an essay from someone else, which is known as 'contract cheating', and this is likely to get you expelled from university. I'll cover each of the major categories of academic misconduct in a moment.

At university we take copying, in any format, really seriously and it comes under a banner called Academic Misconduct. Universities will check you've written your work yourself, and that you've given credit to the people whose work you've used (using something called Referencing).

Academic misconduct is serious, and it is a growing problem in universities, due to students having so many additional pressures competing for their time and attention, amongst other reasons. We do understand the struggle, but we will penalize you for academic misconduct because it's a serious offence to steal another person's work. So, make sure you learn what academic misconduct is, and how to avoid it.

The penalties for academic misconduct can range from a warning or a marking reduction to being asked to repeat a year or being expelled from university. We don't want to do any of these things, so please keep in mind any information you read here, and anything that you read in other Study Skills books as well as information you get from your tutors.

There will be a university policy on academic misconduct, and often information is given to you via Study Skills classes, along with recommended books. In BOX 6.3 below, write down all the places you can get advice and support around academic misconduct.

BOX 6.3 Academic Misconduct Information and Support

Information	Where it is
University policy on Academic Misconduct	
Study Skills Sessions/resources around Academic Misconduct	
Course information around Academic Misconduct	
Recommended books that can help	

Plagiarism

> *Do your best, but do your research, read books on academic writing.*
> **Jasmine**

Plagiarism is where you copy work from a book, a journal, or the internet, and either don't say where you got it from or forget to put the reference in the text of the work.

We check for plagiarism using something called Turnitin™; it's a piece of software that you will, more often than not, submit your assignments to. If your course doesn't use Turnitin™, just remember your lecturers are also pretty good plagiarism-detectors! Turnitin™ will check your work against everything that's ever been submitted to it, and everything it is connected to on the internet. It should be fairly obvious from this that copying is a bad idea.

What we see is a list of all the sources where there is a match to what you've written. If you have done your own work and not copied, then you/we won't see much, your work will be mostly not highlighted. If you've copied information from other sources then your work is going to look like a bowl of Skittles™, and that's not a good thing.

There are always exceptions; sometimes if you're working in a group then parts of the work will look the same, for example methods in a group experimental project. But you have to remember that your lecturers know when work is supposed to be similar and when it is supposed to be different. Write everything in your own words and follow instructions in group work, and everything will be just fine.

Collusion

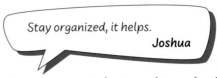

Stay organized, it helps.
Joshua

Collusion is where two or more students work too closely together and then submit the same/similar piece of work. This can happen by accident during group projects where the final piece of work is individually submitted. When you're permitted to work together then go for it; share resources and papers, talk to each other and discuss ideas. But when you write up your work, make sure you write it up alone. It is tempting to all work together on a piece of work, but you do need to resist that temptation. When you are assessed on a piece of work, you are expected to show your understanding and knowledge, not the collective knowledge of your study group or friendship circle. Always write up your work alone.

One big thing to remember is that you should *never* share your assignment with anyone else, no matter what their reason for asking. In collusion cases the person who shares the work is as guilty as the person who copies the work, so both parties will be penalized. No matter how much another student might ask, your answer should always be no. If they ask repeatedly and their communications become negative, contact a member of staff and let them know.

Essay Mills and Buying Essays (Contract Cheating)

> If you cheat or buy essays, you're only cheating yourself.
>
> **Joanne**

Sadly, in recent years there has been a rise in students buying essays from advertised essay mills and sourcing assignments through proof-reading sites which allow free uploads. As of April 2022, the use of these, and the advertising of these services, is now illegal in UK law and will result in serious academic misconduct charges. Often these services will target new students on social media (disguised as support for study resources). The best thing you can do is never discuss your assignments on social media, ignore any contract cheating sites, and block them if they do contact you. You can also access many of the contracted essays for free via Google™. Again, this is on the internet and will be picked up by Turnitin™, whether this is categorized as contract cheating or 'just' serious plagiarism is something that varies between universities. It's always better to *not* use any essays you see for free online.

In addition, we now see assignments generated by artificial intelligence software or students submitting their assignments to free sites to proofread their work for grammar, paraphrasing, etc. All of these options can land you in a great deal of trouble, and universities are constantly updating their guidelines around academic misconduct options. My advice is to avoid using any online services to support the direct writing of your assignments; do the work yourself and ask for help from university services if you get stuck.

We do our best to frame questions so they cannot be answered by essay mill workers, alternative software, and so on, and anyone who does do this is probably going to do pretty badly on the assignment anyway. You need to remember that you are the one who needs to develop the skills we're assessing. If you go into a job where you need the skills we're assessing, if anyone else does your work for you, then you're not going to have developed these skills properly, and you're going to struggle. Make sure you do your own work and you avoid these problems completely.

It might sound like a cliché but by buying an essay, asking someone else to do it for you, or asking artificial intelligence software to do it for you, the only person you will be cheating is yourself. We structure your learning so that you build on knowledge. You are here to do a degree, so do it. It's not easy, but it's a degree, of course it's not easy. However, it's absolutely worth it when you graduate with a huge amount of knowledge and understanding of your subject as well as key skills which will set you up for success in a professional environment.

Paraphrasing and Referencing: How to Avoid Academic Misconduct

Always leave time for proofreading.
Matthew

It's really easy to avoid academic misconduct. Firstly, by doing the work yourself, but secondly by not making mistakes when you make notes and write your work. We want you to write your own work, we know you can copy from other people, so we're not assessing that. We want you to answer the question, and if you copy material from elsewhere you're not going to do that very well.

Paraphrasing is rewording something that someone else has written. For example, I could paraphrase the previous sentence to say:

'If you reword something another person has written, this is called paraphrasing.'

They say the same thing but slightly differently; crucially, the paraphrased version demonstrates understanding.

You need to paraphrase/reword everything you read and make notes on. But you also need another step, **the reference**. This is where you credit someone else with thinking up that information. You will get taught to use particular styles of referencing at university, but they all have the same purpose and major components. In your assignment, you need **WHO** wrote the information first and **WHEN** they wrote it. At the end of your work, you will also add **WHERE** it can be found. So, for my paraphrased statement above, it would look like this:

If you reword something another person has written, this is called paraphrasing (Parson, 2023).

VANESSA'S TOP TIPS
for avoiding academic misconduct

> 'Clever' words aren't essential. Say it as it is.
> **Kaylie**

Here are some quick tips for avoiding academic misconduct:

- Read to understand, not to copy.
  - If you can't write your notes without looking at the page, you don't understand it, so read it again.
- Don't copy when you write notes.
  - Make sure you write down where you got the information from.
- Don't just copy your notes into your assignment.
  - Make sure you answer the question, and that means reframing your notes so they make sense in *that* context.
- If you use information that someone else wrote, say **WHO** wrote it and **WHEN** they wrote it.

Do that every time you use information from somewhere else, and you'll get the hang of it pretty quickly, particularly if you access the guidance from your university and get hold of a good study and referencing guide. Just make sure that when you take notes, you avoid copying what is written/said in the original source as far as possible. Never copy and paste information with the intention to paraphrase it later, you can guarantee one day you'll forget and that will lead to potential problems.

How Not to Mess up Your Degree (and What Happens if You Do)

No question is a stupid question, just ask!
Kathy

Turn up, get involved, do the work. It sounds so easy, but of course it's never that straightforward. Not everyone is happy to chuck themselves head first into university; for some it can be an intimidating process. Equally, not everyone is happy to do lots of reading and work hard all the time. And then there are the students who just love to party!

What you need to remember is that your lecturers were once in your shoes: new students, nervous, unsure what to do or how to write their assignments, wishing we were in the pub instead of class, and a really large proportion of us didn't actually like doing presentations either! Almost all of us do remember what it was like, including the big nights out, so we do understand. But we know you can get through the early nerves and lifestyle adjustments, just like we did. So that's why we keep pushing you to try a bit harder.

Classes can be intimidating, but there is only one way to get comfortable with them—join in. Doing assignments can be a struggle, it's true, but again, there's only one way to get better—read the feedback you're given and try again next time. The main thing is to not give up, and always believe you can do better.

If you do struggle, for any reason at all, be that just understanding an assignment or if there is a more serious issue worrying you, then make sure you get in touch with us. We are all here to support you during your time at university, but we can only help if we know there is a problem. In Chapter 13 we will look at what to do when something goes really wrong. Just remember to talk to us and ask for help if you need it.

And if you are one of those students that likes to party a lot, read the chapter on socializing carefully (see Chapter 11) for some tips about how to balance things. We don't want to stop you having fun, but we do want to make sure you do well in your degree, because that is the reason you're here after all.

A Final Word

Read. Read. Read. A lot of people think they can get through uni without doing independent reading. They're wrong. If you want good grades and want to make things easier for yourself, do some independent reading on subjects you enjoy. Trust me, it will help in the long run.

Rhiannon

Learning to study at university is a lot of fun and can be very exciting, but it can also feel very different from how you've studied up until now. Don't worry, by the end of your first year, you will have got the hang of it. So, turn up, work hard, stay organized, and make sure you do the reading. And whatever you do, remember to do all your own work and ask for help if you need it.

www.oup.com/he/parson1e

Visit the online resources where you will find additional materials including guides on time management, financial planning and budgeting, mindfulness and mental health, hints and tips, as well as all the tables from the book.

Chapter 7

ACCESSING UNIVERSITY SUPPORT AND LOOKING AFTER YOUR MENTAL HEALTH

Why This Chapter Is Important

- Students come to university with a wide range of support needs, and there is support in place to enable students to actively participate in their degrees as fully as possible. Knowing how to access this support is important.
- University is a key transition point in your life, for students from all backgrounds, and with all support needs. Giving you the tools to manage any stress and anxiety that comes with this transition is one of the main reasons for this book.
- There is an increasing awareness of the complexity of life events which impact students, so support for students is now a high priority at universities. Knowing how to access this help is crucial in order for you to feel supported during your degree.

> *Don't be afraid to ask for help, from peers and staff, as there are plenty of people there to support you.*
>
> **Stacey**

Every major transition point in our lives can potentially impact our mental and physical health. This chapter is for anyone with an existing diagnosis of any kind, anyone who is finding the transition to university intimidating or challenging, anyone who might not have the support they need at home or who has a challenging home life, anyone who feels they're struggling to find their place and fit in, anyone who's going through some big changes in addition to starting university, and for everyone who thinks they're going to be just fine, but who may run into difficulties later on.

But most of all this chapter is for you, the person reading this book, because no matter what your circumstances are now, university is going to change your life. I sincerely hope you are one of the students who sails through your degree without any problems at all, but in my experience this is becoming rarer as the pressures of modern life conflict with the desire to study and achieve your potential.

Take the COVID-19 pandemic as an example; this had a huge impact on student mental health, and created one of the biggest pressures we've seen in decades. The international collective trauma, as well as the intense personal circumstances many individuals experienced, has impacted students and staff since 2020. In addition to the impact on mental health, one of the biggest health implications stemming from the COVID-19 pandemic is the condition of Long COVID. We are still learning how to manage this challenging condition as we learn more about the condition itself, and it is very much something that we are expecting to support students with during their studies in the upcoming years. Be reassured that universities are already well adapted and prepared to support students with needs directly related to the COVID-19 pandemic through a whole range of existing policies and procedures.

Events in our lives can impact everything we do, so while you're at university there are a whole raft of resources available to support you during your time with us. This chapter will look at support for mental well-being, support for those with an existing mental health diagnosis or those who are diagnosed with a mental health condition during their studies, and support for those with an existing physical disability. The teams within universities often deal with the support needs of all students so the point of contact is usually the same, but as always it is worth checking if this is the case at your institution (see BOX 7.1).

Support Services Available at University: Identifying Who Can Help You

> *The sooner that you admit that you do need a little bit of support and you do need help. . .the easier it's going to be in the long run*
> **Louise**

Almost everyone needs support at some point in their university journey and it's a sign of strength that you are able to ask for this help. If you are arriving at university with some pre-existing support needs, or you go through a period where some extra support would be useful (even if you don't really know what that support might look like), ,make sure you reach out to the teams at your university and ask for an appointment. They will be able to discuss what support options are available to you.

In BOX 7.1 you'll see some common support services available and where to make a note of all numbers and email contacts you might need, with a few extra blank spaces if your university has additional (or slightly differently worded) support services available to you. If you're not sure where to look, try the student handbook provided by

BOX 7.1 Support Services and Core Contacts Inside my University

Support Service	Email	Phone Number
Security Services/Safety Team		
Campus Police		
Welfare Adviser		
Student Counselling Service		
Well-being/Support Adviser		
Mental Health/Support Adviser/Team		
Disability Support/ Enabling Team		
Finance Support		
Study Skills/Academic Skills Support		
Students' Union		
Equality and Diversity Support		
Chaplaincy (covers all religious faiths and communities)		
Other University Religious Contacts		
Programme Leader/ Director		
Personal Tutor/Personal Development Tutor		
Another Lecturer I know/ trust:		

your university and search for the list below through your university website. Often putting the word 'support' into your university website search page is enough to get you to the core pages on the website with the information you need.

Many students don't like the label 'disability', so not all universities use it; some call it an 'Enabling' team, others use the phrase 'Disability and Inclusion'. What you need to remember is that all services have to be called something, and within these services, we cover all the official 'protected' characteristics, including dyslexia, dyscalculia, all mental health disorders, and of course all physical disabilities. Don't be put off by the label, you are always seen as an individual who simply requires some extra support during your studies, which the highly skilled teams will do their best to provide for you.

There will be many societies and communities within university that can offer support, so think about the types of communities and support services you would find helpful and look for those on the university website. There are more spaces in the appendix for you to add all the support options your university provides.

What You Can Expect from Mental Health and Disability Support at University

Don't be scared to go to the [support] services at the university, they are all really nice people. . .they're there to help and support you

Alice

It is now a key priority for universities to support students with physical and mental health challenges who need some extra support to complete their studies to ensure equal opportunities for all individuals. There are lots of services to assist those with existing support needs while they're at university and you'll find there are teams of very experienced staff available to talk to you and make sure you have the necessary support in place to complete your degree.

If you have an existing diagnosis and you want to ask about what support can be put in place for you before you arrive, contact the Student Support teams ahead of starting. Most universities now ask for declarations of disabilities and disorders when you register, so if you have an existing disability/disorder, I recommend disclosing it to your university. This way, any support you need can be put in place before you arrive, saving you both time and stress. For those students with an existing, or suspected, diagnosis of a mental health disorder, a bit of extra support can go a long way. What I consistently find amazing is how little support some students with really complex profiles need in their day-to-day studies.

If you do not have an existing diagnosis but find that you need support at any point during your degree, then it's important to remember that the first step to accessing support is recognizing that you need it. Once you cross that bridge, you need to go and talk to someone about getting some help; take a friend with you if you need some moral support. Remember that people working in the support services are likely to have seen the full range of difficulties and support needs (and every combination) that individuals can have, so rest assured there are trustworthy and experienced people available to support you during your studies.

One thing to bear in mind is that where there are support needs that the university cannot cover within their established team of specialists, you will be directed to external organizations that work with universities to support students. This is not about moving you to another service; you will still be able to access the support within the universities. Rather, university support teams have a particular range of expertise, so they sometimes have to work with external organizations (e.g. the NHS, Mind, and local organizations) who can provide expertise in other areas to ensure you get the best possible support available during your time at university.

In many universities, your tutors will also be told of your support plan so that they can appropriately support you in your studies, but your details will NOT be widely shared; only staff directly teaching you will have access to support information, and it is always treated as confidential material.

Types of support you might be eligible for depending on your requirements (remember, this varies between universities) are as follows:

- Extra time in exams (usually 25%):
  - Potentially, accessibility facilities such as a computer, a separate room, close location to a bathroom, and a scribe (called an amanuensis), depending on your needs.
  - You might also be eligible for additional breaks with time added on at the end, to accommodate physical disabilities and some health conditions.
- The right to ask for extensions for submitting assignments:
  - If there are no automatic extensions are available, you will still need to contact your Module Leader, but we can often give extensions outside the normal ranges of any policy restrictions in place, giving you that bit of extra accommodation for your particular needs.
- Accessibility elements, such as timetabling considerations:
  - For example, all your classes being scheduled in accessible rooms, advance lecture slides, recordings/transcripts of lectures (although a lot of this is in place as standard practice now).
- Extended library loans.
- Access to funds for specialist equipment to support your learning (including dictation software and specially adapted computers and software).

From September 2020 there was a 'web accessibility' element introduced that is now a legal requirement on all courses, meaning that anything in the online sphere needs to meet minimum accessibility standards. What these standards look like will vary across the university sector, with some universities meeting the standards and others going far beyond the minimum standards. If you want to know what kind of resources we put in place as standard, talk to your new lecturers, recruitment teams, or staff at Open Days events.

With the new legal regulations around web accessibility covering module spaces in the VLE as well as the website, it is getting easier than ever for all students to have accessible options provided regardless of their existing condition, since much of the provision is provided as standard within most modules you take.

Interpersonal Differences: Sexuality, Race, Religion, and Other Demographic Differences

> Be open minded, you'll find a lot of new people who think differently, and have different beliefs to you. Be respectful and treat others and their beliefs how you would want you and yours to be treated.
>
> **Harry**

University is a meeting point for people from all walks of life, and one of the things I personally love about university is how many different demographics, sexualities, cultures, and religions come together with the common goal of learning in a safe and supportive space. While you are at university, we want to ensure you are treated with equity and respect and are able to conduct your learning in a safe and supportive environment without fear of discrimination or being subject to prejudices.

However, we are not ignorant of the fact that there are some common misperceptions, prejudices, and reactions from others which means some students may have negative experiences as a result of not being the same as others. We know that witnessing or experiencing negativity towards interpersonal differences can have a significant impact on your mental health; this is something we want to avoid at university. You should expect to be treated with dignity and respect throughout your time with us, so if this does not happen we want to know so we can support you and address the issue directly.

You may find that your university has a statement on Equality and Diversity on their website and in their policies. Some universities will even have a direct reporting mechanism for anything that comes under the umbrella of Equality and Diversity. Nobody should face any discrimination during their time at university, for any reason.

It is a sad fact that race, skin colour, sexuality, background, and religion often face prejudice and discrimination within society. Within university we do not tolerate discrimination or prejudice of any kind, and we often have reporting procedures in place to support students who do face any kind of discrimination or negative reactions from others during their time with us. It's important to remember that university should be a safe space for all students, from all walks of life and backgrounds. If you do experience or witness any negativity, speak to a member of staff and/or use any anonymous reporting procedures (often visible on university websites within support services provided) that your university has in place.

It is really useful to highlight at this point about the use of personal pronouns such as he/she/they, and titles such as Miss/Mrs/Mr/Mx. When you register for university you will need legal documents regarding name and title. However, we recognize that this is not always representative of how you wish to be seen by your peers and lecturers.

THE POCKET GUIDE FOR STUDENTS

If you have a particular wish to be referred to by specific pronouns, title, or name then please just let us know. We never want to misgender or misname our students, so make sure you are up front and clear about your personal pronoun preferences during your course.

There is a lot of support available so never be afraid to ask for it. As well as the on-campus support services and course contacts listed in BOX 7.1, there are also national helplines to support all individuals with the full range of challenging situations and support needs in Table 7.1. There is a selection of these below, and Student Minds in particular has a wealth of information on their website to help all students throughout their university lives.

Table 7.1 National Helplines and Support Services

Organization	Website	Contact Number
SAMARITANS	www.samaritans.org.uk	116 123 (24 hour)
STUDENT MINDS	www.studentminds.org.uk	Ring Samaritans (see above)
MIND (mental health support)	www.mind.org.uk	0300 123 3393
REFUGE—domestic violence support	www.refuge.org.uk	0800 2000 247 (24 hour)
PAPYRUS—Suicide Prevention Charity	www.papyrus-uk.org	0800 068 4141
ALCOHOLICS ANONYMOUS	www.alcoholics-anonymous.org.uk	0800 917 7650 (24 hour)
NARCOTICS ANONYMOUS	www.ukna.org	0300 999 1212
NATIONAL GAMBLING HELPLINE	www.begambleaware.org	0808 8020 133
RAPE CRISIS	www.rapecrisis.org.uk	0808 802 9999 (to find local services)

Organization	Website	Contact Number
VICTIM SUPPORT	www.victimsupport.org	0808 168 9111 (24 hour)
BEAT—eating disorder support service	www.b-eat.co.uk	0808 801 0677 (adults) 0808 801 0711 (for under 18s)
FAMILY LIVES— parenting support (including bullying)	www.familylives.org.uk	0808 800 2222
RELATE— relationship support	www.relate.co.uk	0300 0030396 (or a local number available on the website)
SWITCHBOARD (LGBT+ support)	chris@switchboard.lgbt	0300 330 0630
THE MIX (support for under 25's)	www.themix.org.uk	0800 808 4994
SANEline (mental health support)	www.sane.org.uk	0300 304 7000
NIGHTLINE	www.nightline.ac.uk	Look for local numbers on website
STONEWALL	www.stonewall.org.uk/	0800 050 2020
MERMAIDS	https://mermaidsuk.org.uk/	0808 801 0400
INTERSEX EUROPE	https://oiieurope.org/	Not a support helpline like the others, but a great resource. See website for more details.
TOGETHERALL	https://togetherall.com/en-gb/	Online Cognitive-Behavioural Therapy. Many universities subscribe to this so that students can access it for free.

Academic Support Available

> If you're having problems in your home/work life don't be afraid to speak to the lecturers.
>
> *Toni*

Not everyone needs to access targeted support and direct intervention, despite the myriad of services on offer. We are aware of this and so there is also academic support, policies, and procedures available that can take into account the fact things may not always go to plan in your life. Often students delay asking for help as they do not want to be perceived as a 'failure' for not meeting deadlines. It is a sign of strength to ask for help, and it is never perceived as a failure in any way. There are policies and procedures around academic support for a reason; don't be afraid to ask for help, we would far rather you ask for help than struggle.

Academic staff might not be able to support you directly with your life events, but we can signpost you to the support you need and we can put in place procedures that will mitigate the impact on your studies. The core thing to remember is that if you are struggling and need some help, for any reason, you should contact your Personal Tutor, Module Leaders, and Programme Leader. There are many options available to us and we can talk you through them as needed. For more information on this, please see Chapter 13.

Look after Your Mental Well-being

> It can be very easy to burn out in higher education, especially if you're thinking of doing a further degree. So, it's important that you work out strategies to manage your stress early on. Talk to your friends and family, and talk to your lecturers! They're there to help and support you.
>
> **Taylor**

Everyone gets nervous when they begin university; it's both exciting and intimidating for all new students, regardless of personal circumstances, age, or experience. There will be exams and assignments to do, you're meeting lots of new people all the time, and you'll be asked to do a lot of things that you might be nervous about (e.g. presentations often cause some anxiety among a few students).

It's really important to remember that it's completely normal to be nervous and anxious; what that tells you is that you care about doing well, that you care about being at university, and that you care about what we think of you. The butterflies and the fizzy feeling in your stomach: those are good things. A few nerves can actually enhance your performance, make you work harder, and push you to achieve more than you ever thought possible.

What can sometimes happen though is that those nerves, feelings of anxiety, and overwhelming emotions become bigger than they need to be, preventing you from engaging with your friends and studies as you would like to. Very occasionally students are overwhelmed to the point where they are potentially at risk of self-harm behaviours, suicidal ideation, and disordered eating patterns—this is rare, but it does happen. The reasons behind spiralling emotions and deteriorating mental health are wide and varied, and there may be an external trigger such as bullying, abuse, or sexual assault. It is important to remember that deteriorating mental health is something that needs to be addressed so that the impact on your long-term health (physical and mental) can be mitigated.

Universities are well aware that there are a great many individuals who do suffer from recognized issues and disorders, such as anxiety, so all universities have support in place that can help you. For more targeted support resources and what to do in particular situations, please see Chapter 13.

Looking out for Your Friends

If you are concerned – speak with staff
Kaylie

You don't just have to look out for yourselves at university, you need to look out for your friends too. Most students will know someone who struggles with mental or physical health issues during their time at university, and sometimes it can be a very difficult situation to navigate. Obviously, you will want be there to support your friends, but sometimes their needs go beyond what you are able to support them with, and they may become seriously unwell, putting themselves and their studies at risk.

It is important to recognize that you cannot always provide the support your friends need, and that sometimes, supporting your friends can put you in an unsafe situation. It is always important to ask for help in such situations. You should, of course, encourage them to contact those sources of support available to them both inside and outside the university. But sometimes they may be reluctant to do so, and this process can be difficult to navigate.

You can support them by offering to accompany them to see tutors and support services, but on occasion you may have genuine concerns for your friends' safety and they may not be in a position to contact anyone for support. When this happens, you should contact a tutor and support services, as well as any external services that are required. All your lecturers will be able to signpost you to the necessary support services, so if you aren't sure who to ask, find a lecturer you trust and talk to them in confidence. None of us will be able to discuss your friend directly with you, but we will be able to contact them directly and try to get support in place for them. All the Tables and Boxes in this chapter (and in Chapter 13) contain the sources of support you need for your friends as well as yourselves; make sure you complete them even if you don't think you personally will need support at university; that way you can quickly help your friends if they need it.

Remember, the most important thing you need to be is their friend and simply be there for them. Sometimes that means helping them get help. In these situations, it is always reassuring for staff and services to see that individuals have support in their lives.

In my 'Top Tips: Spotting the Signs', you will see a list of red flags that can indicate someone might need support from mental health professionals. Read them carefully so that you are well equipped to recognize them and support both yourself and your friends. If you do have concerns about yourself or a friend, make sure you raise them with a lecturer you trust and the support services at your university. These tips have been taken from various resources, including Mind and the American Psychiatry Association.

━━━━━━ VANESSA'S TOP TIPS ━━━━━━

for spotting the signs (recognizing mental health struggles in yourself and others)

> If you struggle with mental health, speak to the disability support team. They're fantastic, they support me in various ways. Also reassuring to know that you're not the only one suffering with mental health at university, I've made friends (surprisingly) through common mental health illnesses.
>
> **Charlie**

- Decrease in daily functioning.
  - Sudden drop in engagement, participation, and performance in daily life and academic study.
  - Finding tasks and academic study disorienting and difficult in a way not normally observed.
- Difficulty thinking and concentrating.
  - Finding basic interactions challenging due to difficulties speaking, remembering, concentrating, and following logical trains of thought.
  - Unable to cope with stress.
- Withdrawal from social connections.
  - Loss of interest in social activities and communications.
  - Social withdrawal that is out of character.
- Mood changes.
  - Rapid or dramatic shifts in emotions that are not necessarily connected with external events.
  - Depressed feelings and mood consistently.
  - Prolonged anxiety and/or feelings of worry.
  - Suicidal ideation.

- Illogical thinking.
  - Unrealistic and/or exaggerated thoughts and beliefs about the self or others, including illogical and magical thinking, or thinking at a level below their chronological age that is not otherwise typical of their cognitive development.
  - Extreme feelings of guilt or worthlessness.
- Increased or decreased sensitivity.
  - Notable change in sensitivity to sensory stimulation and avoidance of situations that is not otherwise explained (e.g. through pregnancy and changes in sensory sensitivity).
- Nervousness.
  - Displaying changes in level of distrust and suspicion of others.
  - Demonstrating uncharacteristic levels of nervousness around others.
- Sleep and/or appetite changes.
  - Sustained changes in regularity, amount, and quality of sleep.
  - Sustained changes in appetite.
  - Decline in, or heightened obsession over, personal self-care.
- Apathy.
  - Lack of desire and initiative to participate in events, activities, or interactions.
- Unusual behaviour.
  - Behaving in a way contrary to normal patterns that is odd, uncharacteristic, and possibly peculiar, which cannot be explained through alternative explanations.
  - Substance use and abuse.
  - Hallucinations.

It's Not Always Plain Sailing: How to Cope with Stress and Pressure

> *From personal experience, don't let this fester, and make sure you talk to someone—family and friends aren't always an option or the best choice, but bear in mind your lecturer will be willing to listen and help you with anything that's troubling you if they can, or point you in the direction of someone who can help.*
>
> **Cassie**

Much like anything that is important to you and requires sustained time, effort, and engagement, there will potentially be periods of stress and pressure during your degree years. You will encounter lots of deadlines, exams, presentations (group and/or individual ones), and many situations that can be stressful for short periods. While there is a lot of support available to you, not all students make use of this because they feel that it's focused more on mental health and physical disabilities.

It's important to remember that stress *is* a mental health issue, so periods of intense stress that you can't cope with *are* something you can go and seek support for. If in doubt, talk to your Personal Tutor and the student support teams. Remember that if you are stressed, you need to find a way to have some space, to take a break—even if that's only an hour. There are some relaxation techniques listed in the 'Anxiety and Stress Help Zone' towards the end of this chapter.

Time management and organization are going to be some of your most important tools when it comes to dealing with stress and pressure. Make sure that you are organized, because once you're in control of your schedule, you will feel more in control of many of the elements within university that can create stress.

While it can be very challenging if you have family and jobs to juggle alongside university, making sure you know what is coming is one of the best ways to avoid stress about completing your course. If you know when deadlines will appear, you can avoid leaving everything until the last minute and becoming stressed as a result.

Resilience and Grit

> *If things aren't going the way you'd hoped. . .don't give up on the end goal, because you will get there.*
>
> **Sarah**

Resilience is the psychological state, or quality, that allows you to pick yourself up when things go wrong and to keep going. People who are resilient don't give up when things go wrong, they find a way to process the events logically, emotionally heal, and adapt their trajectory through life to accommodate anything that has changed. Grit is a key component of this (Duckworth, 2017): it's that perseverance, determination to succeed, to work hard, and to practise.

Neither resilience or grit is something we are necessarily born with; both are attributes that can be developed through focus and practice. Some of the most resilient and 'gritty' people you know achieved their resilience the hard way, through experience of adversity and setbacks. They didn't allow those experiences and setbacks to stop them achieving their goals: they paused, took the time to think and process, regrouped, formulated a new plan, and carried on.

The key component of both resilience and grit is something called a growth mindset (Dweck, 2015), where we don't assume that we have a fixed way of moving forwards, nor a fixed way of learning and achieving our goals; we see opportunities for development and learning and are able to adapt to new situations. A fixed mindset is where we assume that we have only one way of learning, developing, and so on,

161

and is something that can actively inhibit academic study. We don't learn in one way, just like we can't avoid bumps in the road on our path through life. Actively adapting to the challenges around us, which are inherent in everyone's lives to different degrees, is a key component of success at university.

It is entirely normal to experience some stress and a sensation of pressure during your academic studies, and accepting this at the outset means you will be better prepared to deal with it when it occurs. Everyone will experience multiple deadlines and the pressure of a final year dissertation or project; they are fairly standard components of all degrees. Forewarned is forearmed.

Feeling Homesick

> About week 8 into term, I freaked out with extreme homesickness (major panic attack) and my dad drove over in the middle of the night to talk to me. He told me to embrace differences and look at them as opportunities to learn. I did just that and the following day my housemate introduced me to her spice tin from home and taught me to cook a dahl—I have been cooking a mean one ever since.
>
> **Alison**

It's commonly acknowledged that an increasingly large proportion of students go to university close to home, with many staying at home throughout their degrees. Gone are the days when the majority of students left home and didn't see their families again until vacation periods. With so many more mature students, widening participation, and many more financial considerations, the student demographic has changed considerably in recent years.

But there are still a significant proportion of students who do leave home and who are separated from their families during term time. Even with our increasingly digitally interconnected world, it can still be a difficult time adjusting to new surroundings, new people, and an absence of all things familiar. This particularly applies to all international students who come to the UK to study; negotiating a new country where you may not be a fluent English speaker can be daunting and navigating a new culture far from home can be something of a culture shock.

Most UK universities are home to students from across the world as we have a reputation for high-quality higher education. Frequently there are societies and events set up to facilitate introductions for specific cultures; if it helps you, connect with others from your culture, as this will help ease you through this transition period and help you navigate the transition to a new cultural experience as well as the transition to university study here in the UK.

Often homesickness can strike well after the start of term; it's often not something that is noticed early on as you're on a new adventure. The first couple of months are filled with a whirlwind of events and classes, you're constantly meeting new people and experiencing new things, it can be a lot of fun and very exciting. Then, when everything settles down a bit, homesickness can strike.

At this point, it's important to contact the people you miss but while going home to see everyone, if you able to, can be brilliant, it can also be counterproductive as it might prevent you finding and developing your support network at university. During the first year, you're still in the process of transition, and even though it's difficult, you do need to adjust to your new life if it's going to be a success. Set up a call with your family and friends back home, but remember to talk to your new friends at university who will know and understand how you feel (you won't be alone in feeling homesick). Find your support network where you are, this will prove invaluable during the rest of your degree.

Remember, the terms are only a few months long, and you will be home before you know it. In the meantime, focus on your studies and, if you do struggle, make sure you talk to your Personal Tutor.

Extracurricular Activities

Take a bit of time and focus on yourself, if you can't focus on yourself, you'll not focus on your work.

Sarah and Alice

Having extracurricular activities is a great way to ensure you maintain a balanced approach to life. You will find that, along with Student Union Societies (see Chapter 5), the Sport departments often have lots of extracurricular activities available, including on-campus gyms in some institutions. Alongside this, Sport departments may also have initiatives to tackle stress in students. Activity is a great way to reduce stress as it targets the very physical elements connected with our stress response: exercise reduces stress hormones and releases endorphins which are chemicals in the brain that can act as mood elevators.

Of course, you don't just need to access on-site resources, and indeed many students are unable to do this due to childcare and work commitments. Going on walks is very beneficial for physical and mental health, and if you are able to go for walks in green and blue spaces, such as parks, forests, lakes, rivers, and the seaside, you will get the additional benefits of a mental health boost (see World Health Organization resources for more details). Yoga is something you can easily do at home, that supports mental and physical health, with a plethora of online resources and videos available to help guide you.

Look at what options are open to you, what you can do locally to where you live, and what is realistic and within your personal control. But having some extracurricular activities is very beneficial to sustaining good mental health, and it will help you to have a reliable outlet when you are under pressure.

Anxiety and Stress Help Zone

> Do not be afraid to press the pause button, take time out for you, it is so important.
>
> **Emma**

It is important to remember that stress and anxiety are very much a combination of psychological and physiological symptoms. You might find you get breathless when you worry, or you might get stomach ache and feel a bit nauseous. Whatever you feel when you're anxious is a product of your mind focusing on one particular thing too much. Taking your mind away from this one particular thing can help ease your worries and reduce your physiological symptoms. Everyone gets anxious and stressed during at least one period during their degrees, so this section is useful for everyone.

There are lots of mindfulness apps and activities you can try. Here I'm going to list two good activities to try when you're feeling overwhelmed and anxious. Both are based on solid psychological research into mindfulness and anxiety, and you might be familiar with them.

These activities allow you to regain control of your thinking processes, reducing some psychological stress, and give your body the chance to reduce the physiological symptoms related to anxiety and stress. You can use them at anytime and anywhere, whether you're in class, on the bus, or in an exam.

The 5,4,3,2,1 Technique

> *Self-care is one of the most important aspects of university survival.*
>
> **Aimee**

This technique is something of a 'mind hack'; it distracts your mind enough so that you can ground yourself in the present and get some psychological 'space' from your worries, giving you some control over your thinking (see Figure 7.1).

You need to find a series of things in your immediate environment that you can see, hear, touch, smell, and taste. If you mix up the order, that doesn't matter, it's the nature of the exercise that is important.

For example, if I do this right now, I can do the following:

1. **5 things I can see:**
   - My laptop.
   - A cup of tea.
   - Flowers on the windowsill.
   - A bookcase.
   - The cat walking out of the room in disgust that I'm writing instead of giving her my undivided attention!

2. **4 things I can hear:**
   - The sound of the keys on the laptop as I type.
   - The music I've got on in the background.
   - The wind outside.
   - The sound of my breathing.

3. **3 things I can touch:**
   - The laptop.
   - The chair I'm sitting on.
   - The cup of tea.

4. **2 things I can smell:**
   - The flowers on the windowsill.
   - The cup of tea.

5. **1 thing I can taste:**
   - A perfect cup of tea.

Figure 7.1 The 5,4,3,2,1 Technique

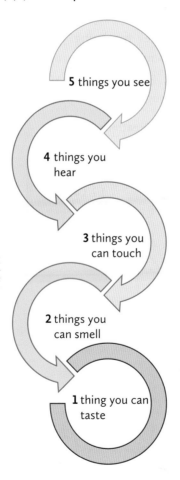

5 things you see

4 things you hear

3 things you can touch

2 things you can smell

1 thing you can taste

It really works, despite all the other things I can see, such as a huge to-do list for my job; just thinking about and writing this list has helped me feel calmer.

Square Breathing

This technique is used in many areas to help calm and quieten the mind and involves regulating your breathing and dealing with the physical elements of stress and anxiety while also giving you something to focus on so you are distracted temporarily from the thoughts you are focused on (see Figure 7.2).

Figure 7.2 The Square Breathing Technique

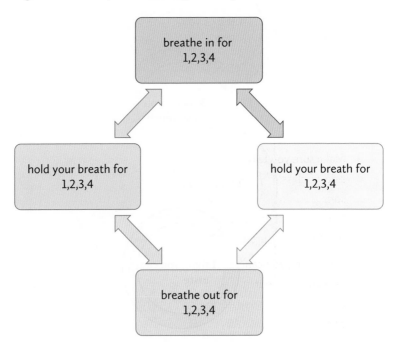

It is very similar to Kumbhaka Pranayama, a breathing technique found in Hatha yoga practice that is known to increase concentration, reduce perceived stress and physiological indicators of stress, and improve mood, as well as having a myriad of other benefits (Jayawardena et al. 2020).

Both square breathing, sometimes called 'Box Breath', and Kumbhaka Pranayama regulate this practice of pausing the breath and enabling the body to pause and focus on the solitary act of breathing instead of the myriad other things that are potentially causing anxiety. The trick to this exercise is to not count too fast, the idea is to count seconds rather than count quickly; you're aiming to slow down your breathing, and allow your body and mind to relax.

VANESSA'S TOP TIPS
for managing your stress at university

> You've got to find head space. . .just take an hour off to do what you enjoy.
>
> **Alice**

Take Things at Your Own Pace

- Make sure you take things at your own pace both inside and outside of class. If you aren't ready to dive in and engage with lessons, stay quiet in class for a little until you're more comfortable. The same goes for social events: it's OK to say no to a few things; don't feel pressured to join in with everything.

- Remember, you can't put off university classes or work or you will fall behind in your studies, so make sure you don't stop working or attending class. If you do find that you're struggling to keep up with things, make sure you access some support and contact your tutors.

Find a Space to Get Some Space

- Focusing on work all the time can mean that you forget about the bits of life you enjoy outside of your studies, which can mean you feel like you're losing bits of yourself; this in itself can make you stressed and anxious, regardless of the number of deadlines.

- It's important to remember that you can't be constantly on the go all the time or you'll end up very stressed, which is something we don't want. Taking a few minutes out to get a coffee or go for a walk is important each day. Make some time for yourself each day and this will positively impact your mental health and reduce your stress levels.

- Find a space where you can take a few minutes to relax and be quiet: it could be a green space, the library, or even a busy coffee shop (some people are more comforted by noise than silence).

- Never underestimate the power of changing your environment to help loosen the grip of a difficult headspace, your environment really does impact how you feel. You might go for a walk, take your laptop and some books to the library or a café, change your room around, or work in a different room in the house. Utilize whatever options are available to you to enable some control over your environment and change it so that you feel less stressed.

Get Some Sleep

- Sleep isn't a magic cure-all but it helps a lot more than many realize. Stress and anxiety can keep you awake, and being tired can magnify feeling stressed and anxious. Many students think working hard and pulling 'all-nighters' will help them catch up, but this is counterintuitive. The reverse is actually true: if you get some sleep, you will work better and more effectively the next day.

Spend Time with Friends

- There is an old saying that goes 'a problem shared is a problem halved'. It's the basis of most therapy. Talk to your friends, close contacts, and family about things that are troubling you. If you feel you cannot talk to friends, find someone within the university who you can talk to, such as support services.

- Make sure you remember to spend time with friends and family; many students focus on work and push their non-university and non-work lives into the corners, only picking them up in the holidays. Make sure you find time to talk to the people you care about regularly, and spend time doing things you enjoy, be that dancing, walking, knitting, or baking. If you enjoy something, make time for it.

- And make sure you remember that your classmates know how you're feeling, so make sure you schedule regular chats with friends from university. Fellow students on your course are the ones who will fully understand your course and its demands, so making course friends early is invaluable at university.

Don't. . .

- Drink too much caffeine: it is a stimulant and will make you feel more anxious. Stick to decaffinated options or reach for water or apple juice instead. Being hydrated will help you stay awake far more effectively than a hit of caffeine that will make you feel *more* anxious. High levels of tea, coffee, or caffeine drinks can play havoc with anxiety *and* your sleep patterns as they can push up the stress and anxiety response and prevent you getting enough sleep. Canned caffeine drinks are particularly bad as they have very high levels of caffeine, often incorporating large amounts of sugar. Remember, chocolate also can contain caffeine, as can many soft drinks.

- Taking in less caffeine, with none after 6 p.m. will help promote healthy sleep patterns and reduce caffeine-related anxiety. Getting enough sleep means much lower stress levels.

• Put off starting your assignments. Delay will lead to more stress and anxiety, not less. If you're stuck and worried, ask for help immediately, don't put it off.

A Final Word

> *Never be afraid to ask for help, you'd be surprised how many are in the same boat.*
>
> SB

Within university we try to ensure that all our students are safe, accepted, and able to access learning during their time with us. There is a lot of support available at university, and it's available to everyone who needs it. It is important to remember that if you feel you need support, for any reason, that you ask for it.

 www.oup.com/he/parson1e

Visit the online resources where you will find additional materials including guides on time management, financial planning and budgeting, mindfulness and mental health, hints and tips, as well as all the tables from the book.

References

Duckworth, A. (2017). *Grit: Why Passion and Resilience Are The Secrets to Success*. Vermillion

Dweck, C. (2015). 'Carol Dweck Revisits The Growth Mindset'. *Education Week*, 35(5), 20–24.

Jayawardena, R., Ranasinghe, P., Ranawaka, H., Gamage, N., Dissanayake, D., & Misra, A. (2020). 'Exploring The Therapeutic Benefits of Pranayama (Yogic Breathing): A Systematic Review', *International Journal of Yoga*, 13(2), 99.

Chapter 8

JUGGLING THE PERSONAL AND PROFESSIONAL SIDES OF YOUR LIFE

Why This Chapter Is Important

- Life doesn't stop when you go to university, all students have to juggle with the personal and academic sides of their lives during their degrees. This chapter is here to help you navigate this balancing act.

- Time management is a skill best learned early, and if you're not already the ringleader of your own circus, now is the time to become that. This chapter has a big section on time management to help you navigate the multiple things you will need to do at university, as well as fit your studies into the rest of your lives.

> You'll find a way to juggle everything.
> **Alice**

The majority of university students now face a wide range of challenges within their lives: balancing additional demands alongside their courses. With increasing numbers of students having part-time (and sometimes full-time) jobs, needing to take account of religious observances and considerations, and engaging in the balancing act that comes with having caring responsibilities, it is really important that we look at this juggling act as a separate topic. There is a big 'Time Management' section towards the end of this chapter, so if you're someone who could use a few extra tips to help you avoid procrastinating and get organized, make sure you read it.

But for most students, engaging with university is going to take some serious organization and motivation. Like all aspects of life, attending university is a balancing act, and often one that is added into already complex lives; this chapter will help you navigate that and show you some options for when things get tricky. The student quotations are important in this chapter, they are all from students who have juggled multiple aspects of their lives during their degrees, and they have some great advice for you.

Work Schedules vs Class Schedules: Juggling a Job and Your Degree

> Go for part time work—you won't have time to work full time on top of a full-time degree. I worked throughout my entire degree, and I found it easy to manage, just be transparent with your employer about your university schedule and deadlines and they can try to help you out.
>
> **Taylor**

Most students will need to manage the tricky balancing act of working alongside your degree classes. This might be occasional shift work, or it could be regular part-time hours that take up considerable time during the week. Juggling this on top of your studies can be very challenging, but it's not insurmountable. Students graduate every year after having balanced work, families, and studies: you will be able to do this too.

It is important to remember why you're coming to university: to get a degree and improve your work prospects after graduation. Yes, earning a living is very important, and you need to make sure you can pay your bills and put food on the table, but you still need to find a way to prioritize your studies. Think long term, not short term.

The first thing you should do is discuss your academic plans with your line manager or supervisor at work. Let them know that you are doing a degree and ask if they can support you by adjusting your hours so they fit around your studies and any other commitments you might have (such as childcare). When you get your timetable, and if you have the option to, discuss this with them and see if you can negotiate shifts that fit with your academic life.

Sometimes, shifts can't be adjusted to suit, for many reasons, so the next step is to talk to your course team, the Programme Leader in particular, and/or the timetabling service at your university. Ask if you are able to adjust some seminar or workshop classes to suit your shifts. While there is a limit to what we can do when it comes to the timetable, there are usually multiple classes running for seminars and workshops so there is often some flexibility here. Most universities are happy to adjust your timetable to suit your external commitments if they can. In BOX 8.1 you can complete the contact details of the people you need to contact about timetable concerns.

However, one thing we can't move is lectures. There is often only one instance of these, so there might not be an alternative. In this situation, you need to discuss options with your course team—speak to your Programme Leader and see what they suggest. My advice here

BOX 8.1 Timetabling Queries

Person/Service	Contact Information/Email
Timetabling	
Programme Leader	
Module Leader	
Personal Tutor	

is to make every effort to attend. While they may be recorded, there is no substitute for being there in person, and you will gain a valuable understanding of your subject by hearing your lecturers speak live and being able to ask questions.

We are aware that not everyone has ideal working conditions, and while we do expect you to prioritize your degree, we are not ignorant of the fact that many of you (and potentially your family) rely on that income. Where you are really struggling to fit everything into your week, make an appointment with your Personal Tutor and have a chat with them to see what options are available to you.

With blended/hybrid learning and online courses, there is an in-built flexibility with sections of the course being self-directed study and independent learning focused. As a result, it is often slightly easier to juggle external commitments around those classes you do need to attend on campus and/or online as they are typically the seminars and workshops that may have repeat sessions and you can ask your Programme Leader or the timetabling team to switch sessions. But for online or blended/hybrid learning courses, don't forget that there will still be some elements that you will need to attend at a specific time, be that face-to-face (F2F) classes or 'Live Virtual' classes; you should make sure that you can attend. It is even less likely that you will be able to adjust your timetable in 'live' class instances, so plan ahead and let your line manager or supervisor at work know well in advance that you will be absent on those days/times.

In BOX 8.1 you will find a list of the important people you need to get in touch with for all your timetabling and work juggling needs inside university. Write down this information and make sure you contact them if you need to ask for adjustments and/or support.

Family Life and Caring Responsibilities

> *You may feel selfish for putting yourself and your university experience first, but don't. You will benefit your child(ren) in the long run. If your child is old enough, explain how important it is that they give you some space to work. My five-year-old likes to do her homework while I do mine!*
>
> **Aimee**

As I've already mentioned, the demographics of the student population are changing, and we have many more mature students embarking on their degree adventures now. Since 'mature student' is anyone over the age of 21, this can encompass a wide variety of living situations, which I'll cover in greater depth in Chapter 9. In addition, partly as a result of successful widening participation initiatives, students who are not classified as mature students may also have family and caring commitments. As a result, many students at university now have caring responsibilities, looking after their own children, siblings, or other family members. It is not easy juggling these responsibilities, so it takes a bit of extra effort to reorganize your life to encompass your new academic role.

Remember too that your lecturers know how all-encompassing academia can sometimes feel. It can be intimidating to share personal information with your tutors, who can sometimes seem unapproachable, but you'll find many of your lecturers and tutors are also parents or carers; juggling academia with family life is something we already do, and we are well aware of the challenges involved. Don't be afraid to talk to your tutors if you find it difficult to balance things.

Childcare

> *Plan childcare early, have a plan before you get to uni, this saves on stress and worry.*
>
> **Adam**

A big consideration for those who have children is finding suitable childcare: family support, nursery places, school breakfast clubs, and after-school clubs or childcare are crucial to finding time to get to class and complete your studies. You should get your timetable when you enroll, but often this is too late for organizing formal childcare and school breakfast or after school clubs, which have to be organized well in advance (often as early as April/May).

Not all students have partners and/or grandparents/relatives nearby who can help out with childcare. You might be a single parent, your partner might work away, there could be a wide variety of reasons why you can't ask your closest relatives nearby who can help, or you might not have any family who can help at all. All of these things mean you need to get a headstart on planning.

You will usually have have three options with regards to timetables:

1. Contact your Programme Leader directly and ask how you can adapt your timetable, within reason, to suit your caring commitments. This is the best option once you have your timetable, as your Programme Leader will have been involved

in creating the timetable so will know what you can (and can't) shift, and the implications that will have for you.

2. Once you get your timetable, contact the timetabling team direct (the email address is often on the main 'splash' page of the website, and in the early materials you receive) and ask to move seminar/workshop groups. It's unlikely that you'll be able to move lectures unless there are repeats (sometimes this is the case on really big courses).

3. Contact your Programme Leader *before* you register/enrol to ask about when your classes are. Timetables are generally ready by around May/June as staff need to plan for the upcoming academic year, so your Programme Leader will be able to give you some information about which days you are likely to need childcare. They might not be able to give you exact details, but they are likely to be able to offer enough details for you to organize childcare. Then, when you get your timetable, if there are any issues, just send your Programme Leader and/or timetabling team an email.

Keeping All The Plates Spinning

> *Get a big family calendar. University isn't forever, it's a stepping stone to have a better life.*
>
> **Nickayla**

One of the things that students with caring responsibilities have in common is the number of things they have to effectively try to do at once. You have to care for your children/relatives, work, go to university, complete your academic work and submit all your assignments, and spend time with your partners and wider family (if they form part of your daily lives). And in amongst all that you have to sleep, eat, and take care of yourselves. It's a lot to do and keep track of.

Caring commitments are a big chunk of what you need to do and they are absolutely your priority. Planning your time is important (see Time Management below), but adaptability, flexibility, and resilience are also going to be critical skills during your time at university. Luckily, those with caring commitments tend to already have good doses of all these attributes before they get to university, and their studies are just another plate among the many others they're trying to keep spinning.

One of the biggest tips I can give all those with caring responsibilities is to take advantage of time between your classes. While you're at university, all the caring commitments are under control and you have time to yourself to focus on your studies. Definitely make time to grab a coffee with friends but make sure you get to the library and study as well; take advantage of this quiet time where you can focus on your studies, it's a precious commodity.

It's also worth knowing that there are some big advantages to how university learning works, in contrast to formal learning prior to university. Outside of classes, you can organize your learning time to suit you and your family. If you want to get up an hour earlier to get some reading done, go for it. If working later at night when everyone is asleep works better for you, make sure you do it. Organize your time outside class to suit you and your family, that way you won't feel like you're letting anything slip at home while you study.

However, as with all things in life, one extra thing to do can sometimes be all it takes to make it all fall apart. Making sure you adapt your time carefully and avoiding burnout is more important when you have others dependent on you. Finding time for yourself is crucial, so if that means that you need to ask for an extension because one of the kids has been up all night and you need a nap more than you need to submit a sub-standard piece of work the next day, you should talk to your tutors as quickly as possible.

Time Management

> Break things down into manageable chunks, almost like a plan of attack. Know how much you want to get done each day, but still build in time to do things for yourself.
>
> **Lizzie**

I'm fairly sure you know you will need to manage your time while you're at university, so this section is to reinforce the importance of this and to give you some handy tips that will help you, and hopefully prevent you from leaving everything until the last minute. If you're already an organizational whizz, that's brilliant; hopefully, this section will help hone your skills. If you're generally not quite as organized as you might like to be, then this section is definitely one to read carefully. Being organized can make a big difference to your time (and performance) at university.

VANESSA'S TOP TIPS

for time management

> At first it may seem daunting but managing the workload starts to become more natural, as time goes by it becomes much easier as you develop skills and knowledge with help along the way.
>
> **Jamie**

- Plan ahead.
- Use a diary or calendar.
- Expect the unexpected.

Plan Ahead

I cannot emphasize this one enough: if you work in advance of your deadlines, they don't all appear at once and overwhelm you, making your university journey so much less stressful for you. Work out when your deadlines are and make sure you write them down. That way you can plan your time and work out what you need to do, and when it needs to be done by.

If you need additional support, for example assistive software or direct disabled student support, then make sure you plan ahead for accessing this support and making full use of it. As we covered in Chapter 7, there is a whole suite of support available for those who need it; if you think that you might need some support, make sure you get that support in place as early as possible.

Use a Diary or Calendar

Most phones now include an integral calendar, along with the option of notifications to remind you to do things. You can even create multiple calendars for the different aspects of your life, colour coding different elements such as family, work, and university. Some digital calendars, like Google Calendar, allow you to share your calendar with others—particularly useful if you are sharing childcare or caring responsibilities with someone else. Use the calendar in your smartphone, or via an app; they're an invaluable resource and an absolutely brilliant way to keep organized. They can tell you when things are due to happen, and you can set notifications up to remind you what you're doing next.

If you prefer a paper diary, then ensure you keep it up to date; use sticky paper notes and coloured pens to make sure that everything is clear. Wall calendars work really well too, they give you a nice clear overview of your academic year, so you can see where it gets busy and where you can afford to take a bit of time out to rest.

You can access all kinds of templates online, or create your own. During term time a weekly planner is a great idea, it can help you keep track of all the things you need to do and stay on top of everything.

Essentially you need to work out your preferred method of organizing your university schedule and use it to get yourself into a routine. If you can crack staying organized in your first year at university, you're probably going to stay on target throughout your degree. Use whatever method suits you best and stick to it.

In BOX 8.2 is an organizational check list that you can use to check off things you can do that will keep you organized. Schedule in non-academic and work activities too; you will need to find time for grocery shopping, socializing, laundry, extra-curricular activities, the school run; you need to find time for everything that goes on in your life. I've added extra spaces for you to write in anything else that you can think of that you need that will help you stay organized.

BOX 8.2 Organization Check List (Tick All That Apply)

I know how to use the calendar in my smartphone or app	
I know how to set alerts for myself	
I have a separate calendar I can put on my wall	
I have my class timetable	
I have put my class timetable in my calendar	
I know when my assignments are	
I have put my assignment deadlines into my calendar	

I have put my work shifts into my calendar	
I have put my child's schedule into my calendar (if applicable)	
I have put my student card somewhere sensible where I won't lose it	
I know who to contact if I'm running late (see BOX 8.1)	

Probably the most important BOX to complete is BOX 8.3. This is somewhere to list all your deadlines for the next academic year. Fill it in and refer to it throughout the year if you get stuck. There's another version at the back of the book as well.

Expect the Unexpected

As we all know, life doesn't always go to plan, and during the course of your degree, you will need to adapt to changes that occur in your life pregnancy, loss, illness, financial changes, work changes, family dynamic changes, even housing changes can all have an impact on your studies. The trick is to plan in advance to ensure that your schedule is flexible enough to manage any unexpected situations that appear. Learning to adapt and not panic is an important skill. Use the tips I share in Chapter 7 around stress relief, reorganize your schedule to suit the changes, and contact your lecturers if the impact of the unexpected event is bigger than you feel you can manage.

BOX 8.3 Your Deadlines

Module	Assignment	Deadline	Have I Put This Deadline in my Smartphone/Diary/ Wall Calendar?
			Yes/No
			Yes/No
			Yes/No
			Yes/No
			Yes/No
			Yes/No
			Yes/No
			Yes/No
			Yes/No
			Yes/No
			Yes/No
			Yes/No
			Yes/No
			Yes/No

Procrastination and Motivation

As a massive procrastinator myself, I would try to advise you to not leave [assignments to the] last minute.

Alex

Let's talk about procrastination for a moment: are you any good at it? I'm amazing at it; you should see the amount of things I've done (or not) while I've been writing this book! What you need to do at university is manage any tendencies you have towards procrastination, and help yourself focus on your work. Find whatever tricks work for you (see the Top Tips in this section for some ideas) then use them.

Around assignment deadlines, you're going to want to be a bit extra organized, and one of the things that will help is a digital detox. It's not for everyone, but most of us use our phones far too much. There's nothing wrong with that if it's productive, but if you're trying to write an essay and you keep checking social media, then you're not working hard at all. Read Chapter 12 for more advice on this.

Many students leave their assignments until the last minute, whether that's through stress, procrastination, or other parts of life intervening. Generally, leaving anything until the last minute is really unhelpful—for everyone. Students end up stressed because they don't have enough time to complete work, and your lecturers end up frustrated that you're asking questions we answered in class and emails many weeks ago. Here are some tips that will help.

VANESSA'S TOP TIPS

for completing work on time

> Plan, plan, plan. Set yourself achievable targets and reward yourself upon submission.
>
> **Aisha**

- Work in advance.

  It sounds so simple, but external factors can often impact motivation and lead to your work taking a back seat temporarily. Planning and ensuring you stick to a schedule (see above) is really important to ensure that if and when you get a dip in concentration, you have the work you've already done to fall back on. If you don't work in advance, you may end up feeling panicked like you're behind and don't have enough time to complete your work. This is when we get emails, and it's often too late for us to help much, which is very frustrating for everyone. If you work in advance and pre-empt the fact that you'll have periods of lower motivation. Working in advance also allows you to make incremental progress on big assignments which can help reduce stress later as you won't be starting from scratch, and the task at hand should feel increasingly more manageable.

- Set yourself realistic goals.

Break down the tasks you need to do (e.g. read a paper, find some information for an essay) so that it doesn't feel overwhelming to look at. Working like this means working in advance, and that pays dividends in the long term when it comes to submitting your work on time. If you break down tasks and plan in advance, you can avoid procrastination and the stress that goes with working quickly at the last minute. There are lots of free tools, such as Trello or even Excel, that you can use to plan the steps you need to take in order to achieve your learning goals (e.g. submitting an assignment on time). These planning tools (available online), or even using something as simple as post-it notes or lists, can work wonders when planning and producing your assignments.

- Reward yourself when you complete tasks and assignments!

This is a really useful tool for motivation, something which we can all struggle with at times. It could be a night out with friends, time with your family, or something as simple as a pizza or a bar of chocolate.

Having/Adopting Children During Your Degree

> *Your body will get tired—no academic staff will be bothered if you are a few minutes late to class—they would prefer this over you running across campus tiring yourself out further.*
>
> **Ebony**

Surprisingly often during degree programmes, whether planned or unplanned, babies are conceived or adopted. Unfortunately, they aren't delivered by a stork at a convenient time so you will need to look at the impact the pregnancy and adoption will have on your degree programme. Lots of students gain children (sometimes multiple) during their degrees, and there are policies and processes in place for when this happens.

This section is organized around those individuals who do get pregnant. However, if your partner gets pregnant, you may want to follow some of the same advice so that you can attend ante-natal appointments with your partner. Equally, while this section is oriented around those individuals who conceive, be that naturally or through fertility treatment, some students do go through the process of adoption during their degrees as the time is right for them to do so, for various reasons. If you choose to adopt, and if you are going through fertility treatment, you should follow as much of the advice that applies below as you need to. Make sure the relevant academic contact is aware; this might be your Programme Leader and Personal Tutor, or it might be a dedicated member of university support staff. Making sure they are informed about significant changes on your horizon is crucial to ensure you get the right support while you're at university. I've referred you to your Programme Leader throughout this section, as it is the most typical contact, but apply the same advice if you are directed to another contact to support your academic studies while pregnant. Your Personal Tutor will always need to know.

Pregnancy can be amazing or it can be a challenge, for all sorts of reasons. Morning sickness, pregnancy-related health conditions, and the basic challenge of your belly expanding fairly dramatically all mean that you need to ensure you get the right support. If you're going through fertility treatment, you will have the dramatic hormonal impact to consider, along with a number of appointments for all steps of the process, even before finding out whether your treatment is successful and potentially going through the pregnancy hormone rollercoaster.

You need to follow a fairly consistent set of procedures when you get pregnant, so make sure you follow the list below (and complete BOX 8.4).

1. Let your Programmer Leader know as soon as it is safe to do so, typically around the time of your first ultrasound scan or when you start fertility treatment. If you are happy to let them know beforehand, that is ideal, since it gives us a warning to be prepared for all outcomes as early as possible.

2. Once you have had your first ultrasound scan, confirm your dates with the academic team and complete any paperwork. You will need to take details of the following:

   a. An emergency contact person, their phone number, and relationship to you.

   b. Due date.

   c. Any health-related concerns (e.g. diabetes).

   d. When your Health Visitor and ante-natal appointments are. Ideally, you'll arrange these around your timetable, but where that is not possible, you have a legal right to attend ante-natal appointments, so your Programme Leader will ideally help you adapt to this where your course is concerned.

3. At this meeting your Programme Leader should either complete or organize a Risk Assessment. This is because we need to ensure your safety while you are on campus. Which degree you do will determine what protection and adaptations are needed while you're pregnant. If there are concerns, your Programme Leader should discuss these with you. For most degree subjects, the risks are obvious and minimal, and a risk assessment is a formality.

4. Your Programme Leader will also discuss your options for maternity/adoption leave and your course.

   - When you give birth, there is a compulsory two-week period where you are not allowed back into university or classes, and you are unable to sit exams. You're typically not even allowed on campus itself. This is a government-mandated legal requirement so that you can recover from childbirth. *There are no exceptions*, and you should not expect communication with the university in this time. This is applicable to all births, regardless of the outcome, and is in place so you can recover physically (and mentally) from giving birth.

   - For C-sections, your Programme Leader might require you to get the all-clear from your Health Visitor (typically around six weeks post-birth) before you can return to class, since a C-section is major surgery, and the recovery time is typically longer.

   - If you adopt, there is a mandatory six-month maternity leave required, although without the legally binding two-week period for recovery associated with birth. You will need to ensure that you carefully consider whether you are able to complete your studies alongside this. If possible, consider pausing your studies during this academic year (see point 6).

5. Depending on your situation, your Programme Leader may also refer you to the university Support Services if they feel you would benefit from additional support. If they recommend this, make sure you go (details in Chapters 7 and 13), they will help as far as they are able to.

6. Your Programme Leader will discuss the option of something called a 'Leave of Absence', or 'Suspension of Studies' (see Chapters 9 and 13). Courses are set up to run in a particular way and we can't adapt this to suit individual circumstances. Sometimes it is in your best interests to pause your studies and your Programme Leader can discuss this with you.

During your pregnancy, if all goes well, you should get through it with minimal issues on your course, but make sure you factor in your pregnancy to everything you need to do while on campus, such as getting to class, proximity to bathrooms, and ensuring you eat regularly.

There is mixed evidence for the concept of 'baby brain', however it's widely acknowledged that there is a small reduction in grey matter volume during pregnancy, which then recovers quite quickly after birth (Luders et al., 2020), within around four to six weeks. This may not have any noticeable impact, but you may find it takes a bit longer to complete work. You need to plan extra carefully and give yourself time to complete work, particularly near the end of your pregnancy. Make sure you contact your Personal Tutor if you are struggling to concentrate; they may wish to revisit the plan they put in place during the initial meeting about your pregnancy.

Sometimes students start their course then the adoption and/or fertility treatment plan they'd put on hold for their studies suddenly becomes a current issue and they try to juggle both. Each case is unique, so contact your Programme Leader directly to discuss your options.

BOX 8.4 Starting/Expanding Your Family Checklist

Checklist	Done?	Details
Made an appointment with my Personal Tutor and Programme Leader or Support Contact	YES/NO	
Found (and read) the relevant University regulations or policies (Pregnancy/Maternity and/or Adoption)	YES/NO	
Completed the Pregnancy checklist with my Programme Leader or Support Contact	YES/NO	
Provided emergency contact details	YES/NO	
Discussed the impact of Health Visitor and/or medical appointments	YES/NO	
Discussed any complications that I might have relative to my situation	YES/NO	
Discussed the impact on my course and what my options are (including pausing my studies)	YES/NO	
Thought about how childcare will be organized	YES/NO	
Discussed a risk assessment for my programme of study with my Programme Leader or Support Contact	YES/NO	
Found out what sources of support are available to me	YES/NO	

Occasionally, for reasons that are often unknown, pregnancy outcomes do not result in a happy and healthy baby. It is an incredibly traumatic experience to lose a child, at any stage of pregnancy or following birth.

In the event that you experience miscarriage, stillbirth, or the loss of a child soon after delivery, you should contact your Programme Leader and/or Personal Tutor as soon as you are able to. Just letting them know will mean they can immediately contact everyone who needs to be aware, support you with any forms you need to complete and decisions you need to make, and a raft of support measures can be put in place. These support measures will include access to the Counselling Service, and we can support you getting access to emergency counselling sessions.

In all cases, whether it be pregnancy, fertility treatment, adoption, or loss of a child, ensure you contact the finance team to discuss your options if you need additional support or are taking a break from your studies. There are a range of options for supporting you during your studies, and these are covered in more detail in Chapters 7 and 13, so read these carefully.

Cultural and Religious Considerations

> You will likely never to find a better melting pot of cultures and ideas than a modern university, so take this opportunity to find your own identity and learn to courteously express it whilst learning about the cultures, identities, and traditions of others.
>
> **Cassie**

The UK is a culturally diverse country, with a wide variety of ethnic and religious communities. Culture is a very broad term, one that is defined by social norms and issues, so I'm using it here to refer to those elements of a culture which come with specific observances and considerations, such as fasting, prayer, and observed days of rest/non-work. As the official religion in the UK, which is the religion held by the Monarchy, is Christian, all those observances, and all UK national holidays, are already considered during timetables and semester planning.

For all other religious and cultural observances, it is useful to look at your personal calendar and see what the impact is on your studies. For example, if you are Muslim you may want to consider when Eid and Ramadan fall, and look at what adjustments you need to make to factor in the observances, such as fasting, that are connected with these periods of time.

Spiritual and religious observances are important to a large proportion of students who attend university, and so there is support in place for this. The vast majority of universities have prayer facilities on campus, so make sure you locate and find them before you start university. If you need to pray at particular times of the day, contact your Programme Leader and/or timetabling (see BOX 8.1) to try and adjust classes as far as possible.

You will find there is a Chaplain on site, who is typically an accredited, non-denominational religious individual who supports students of all religious faiths (see BOX 8.5). Don't be put off by the Christian terminology, you are able to contact the Chaplain regardless of religious or spiritual persuasion, and you should find support and understanding. Indeed, you can contact the Chaplain even if you are not religious. Many universities also have additional religious leaders and/or support staff in post, as the religious demographic of the UK is now being considered more carefully in provision available for students.

BOX 8.5 Locations of Prayer Facilities and Religious Contacts

Facility/Contact	Location	Contact Number
Prayer Facilities/ Room		
Chaplain (covers all matters of faith in all religions)		
Other Religious Leader (e.g. Imam)		

The key things to remember are:

1. You should feel supported in following your cultural and religious observances while you're at university.

2. You should not feel intimidated or experience any negative feedback for following cultural or religious observances. If you do, there is advice on how to get support in Chapter 13.

3. Make sure you plan around your particular observances. If you need to schedule in a time to pray each day, make sure this forms part of your daily schedule in your notes and planning, add it in to your smartphone calendar so that it's visibly blocked out each day. Log each cultural and religious event that isn't automatically included in your smartphone calendar. While you will remember, it can help to have a visible section

of time blocked out when you're planning how to fit your university work into your schedule.

Asking for Support

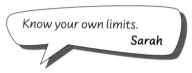

Know your own limits.
Sarah

Juggling all the various aspects of your life can be a big challenge, particularly if you're juggling all of the aspects I've discussed above. Make sure that you don't forget there is support available to you at university should you need it. In Chapter 7 we looked at what your various sources of support are, in Chapter 3 we cover finances, and in Chapter 13 we will cover what happens when something goes wrong, be that in your personal or academic life.

Don't be put off talking to staff if you're struggling to keep up with your coursework because of work or family commitments, and don't be concerned that your lecturers might think you're not prioritizing your studies. As long as you keep communicating with us then we can support you in juggling the various demands in your life.

Nobody expects you to be organizational superheroes when life gets complicated and challenging, so you should make sure that if things get tough, you ask for support. There are lots of situations where you might need a bit of extra help, and I've gone through a wide range of these in Chapter 13, with who to turn to in those situations.

Becoming The Most Organized Version of Yourself

> As a parent of 2 children under 5, it can be very challenging. Making time to sit and study is crucial; if you don't do it you may struggle. I set aside time or days to study after short lectures. If you're already at the university why go home, sit and do some work.
>
> **Charlie**

There's a reason I've focused on organization here, because that's the key to staying on top of everything while you're at university. If you start early, you're prepared, and that reduces worry and stress throughout your studies. If you start early, you have time to ask questions so that you understand what you need to do. If you leave everything until the night before a deadline, you'll end up panicking. Start early, and avoid the panic.

Life after university is going to continue to be a juggling act, so developing your methods for managing this while you're at university will stand you in good stead for the challenges and adventures you'll have once you graduate. While you are at university, work out the best methods for organizing your time, and how to split your time between your different commitments.

Remember, you're aiming for organized, not selfless martyr. It's in nobody's best interest if you work all hours of the day; you need to plan in time for yourself as well. Make sure you have time off, even if you need to program it into your smartphone calendar so you're reminded about it (I do this a lot!).

Making time for yourself can be really challenging, but it's really important so you don't burn out and end up crashing out of university because you feel you can't cope. You can cope, of course you can, and there is plenty of support to help you do just that. But you need to acknowledge that you need to look after yourself as well. Eat well, get sleep, and prioritize effectively.

A Final Word

Become the ringleader of your own circus!
Alice

Juggling work, children, religious and cultural observations, and all aspects of your personal lives takes work and planning. If you start organizing yourself early, things will slot into place very quickly. So, don't put off writing a schedule for yourself, just make sure you stick to it as far as possible. My top tip is to utilize the calendar in your smartphone and reward yourself for getting things done. Then, if life gets a bit complicated and messy, make sure you let your tutors know and ask for some help. As Alice mentions in her quotation, become the ringleader of your own circus (actual juggling optional).

 www.oup.com/he/parson1e

Visit the online resources where you will find additional materials including guides on time management, financial planning and budgeting, mindfulness and mental health, hints and tips, as well as all the tables from the book.

References

Luders, E., et al. (2020). 'From Baby Brain to Mommy Brain: Widespread Gray Matter Gain After Giving Birth', *Cortex*, 126, 334–342.

Chapter 9

HOUSING AND HOUSEMATES

Why This Chapter Is Important

- Students have a wide variety of home and living arrangements. This chapter highlights the key things to consider in each situation to help you balance your home life and academic life.

- All living situations have their own challenges, so key considerations and things that will help are covered in this chapter, along with whom to contact if housing challenges arise.

> *Pay your rent as soon as your student finance comes in—don't wait. You'll end up spending more than you think and could end up short if not.*
>
> *Kallie*

While student accommodations (also known as Halls of Residence in most universities) are still a core part of student housing, the rise in students studying close to home and living with their own families means there is a wider variety of considerations to think about when it comes to housing. I've used the term 'housemates' in the title for this chapter, but that could easily mean your partner, children, or parents/caregivers rather than your fellow students.

In this chapter we'll look at all varieties of housing situation, and I'll provide some advice on studying, social spaces, and what to do when transitioning between different types of living accommodation. I'm not going to give you advice about types of accommodation, the decision is yours, and is often made for you in a great many cases. UCAS has a great set of resources on their website, and your university will have more detailed information about accommodation in their areas. You can also contact your university accommodation team (see BOX 9.1) if you need more advice.

Just remember, housing and associated costs form a significant part of our daily budgets and so there will be times when I refer back to Chapter 2 where we covered finances. Occasionally financial difficulties impact on accommodation, and again, you can use the information in Chapter 2 to guide you in accessing the support you need.

University Student Halls: Noisy and Fun

> Always keep your keys/pass next to a hoody and some trainers because you WILL have a fire drill at 3 a.m. and it won't be warm.
>
> Ling

We'll cover the traditional home of the new student first: university halls, also known as student accommodation or halls of residence. This is often in the form of blocks of flats, with anywhere from two to fifteen rooms/students per floor/corridor. The type of accommodation in halls can vary quite a lot: some provide shared bathrooms, others offer ensuite rooms, and almost all provide communal cooking spaces. While there are still a few catered halls of residence, they're often only in the older universities, so you will find the most common accommodation type is self-catering and it's time to learn how to cook if you don't already know how!

All student accommodation is organized by the Accommodation Office (or similar). You'll find that if you have any questions at all, it is your go-to place. It will have opening hours, so make a note of these, and the contact details, in BOX 9.1.

BOX 9.1 Accommodation Office Contact and Availability Details

Accommodation Office/Residence Office	Key Information
Phone number	
Office/Opening hours	
Email	
Website	
Where it is located on campus/in the halls of residence	
Out-of-Hours contact details	
Location of nearest laundry (this is very important!)	
Wi-Fi details/password	
Technical Support (if available)	

While living in halls can be fun, it can also be quite noisy at times, so it's important to be considerate of your neighbours. If you do want to live on a quiet corridor, or in a quiet part of an accommodation block, then it is worth contacting the Accommodation Office directly when you accept your place to make a request. Some accommodation services will match students together with like-minded students; for example, you can ask to be placed with other students who are LGBTQI+ friendly.

Many (not all) university-owned Halls of Residence now have Wi-Fi. However, it is important to remember that this is a shared Wi-Fi resource and therefore it may occasionally be a little unreliable. Sometimes, Wi-Fi usage is included in the price you pay for your accommodation, which means that often there might be charges if you go over a specified limit of data usage. Some universities do not have Wi-Fi, some do, some limit Wi-Fi usage, and some don't; this information will be made clear in details you get about accommodation charges.

Whatever the set-up, try to limit your use of the internet to work-related activities, and avoid downloading or streaming movies and music. Don't forget, if your Halls of Residence does not have Wi-Fi you have access to the university campus computers as well, and some will be available 24/7, so while you're on campus or in halls you're unlikely to be stuck for access to the internet.

It is also worth checking what other facilities the halls of residence offers: some provide onsite security, launderette, and possibly even cleaners.

Making It Feel Like Home

Fairy lights help with a cosy atmosphere rather than the big strip light being on always.

Lynn

Your halls of residence is a home away from home. It's also your safe space at university, so you need to feel comfortable in your room. While for some students their new accommodation can represent freedom and their own space, for others this new environment, can feel very unfamiliar, which can lead to homesickness for some students. Making sure that you have things around you that are familiar can help you with the transition to living where you are at university.

You will need basic things like a duvet, bed linen, towels, toiletries, clothes, stationery, and potentially cooking equipment/crockery. If you haven't yet moved into your accommodation there are plenty of helpful lists of things to pack for halls that you can find online. But beyond these basics, there are many things you can do to make a fairly functional room a bit more fun and comforting.

Bringing pictures of family and friends, and favourite items you associate with home (although don't take anything from home your relatives will miss!) will all help make your new room look more homely. The lighting can often be less than ideal, so consider bringing fairy lights and lamps to make the lighting softer and more manageable, a particularly useful tip if you suffer from migraines. Don't forget cushions and soft furnishings, books, small (hardy) houseplants, digital equipment such as alarm clocks and portable speakers, and so on.

You want to make sure that you have things around that help you feel a little more settled. It will be very strange for a while, but hopefully you'll make plenty of friends on your corridor. (I'm still friends with a few of the people I shared a corridor with in my first year at uni!)

Living in Halls as a Care-Experienced/Estranged Student

University is such a diverse and inclusive environment which is especially important for care-experienced/estranged students.

Eddy

Often those students coming from a background of care from local authorities come directly into university-maintained Halls of Residence as there are often financial incentives for this (see Chapter 2). If this applies to you, make sure you contact the team within the university that is there to look after and support you during your studies, be that with moving, first food shop, advice, or general support. This might be the general support team, or there might be a dedicated support team (see Chapter 2). It can be a particularly daunting but exhilarating experience being suddenly independent, and you should make the most of support available to you.

Living with Other Students

> *Set up a group chat with your flatmates in case you get locked out.*
>
> **Betty**

What you will need to remember is that you're sharing a living space, so some basic courtesy and consideration is needed. Here are some tips for how to negotiate living with lots of people you don't know (yet).

VANESSA'S TOP TIPS
for living in Halls of Residence

> *Don't leave anything in the kitchen that you would miss if it were stolen/broken/found three weeks later at the bottom of the kitchen sink with mouldy pasta in.*
>
> **Hannah**

- Be considerate.
  - You're living with people you don't know, so try to remember that not everyone will want to live in the same manner as you. Not everyone will want to party, but equally, not everyone will want silence. Find the balance and take the time to learn about your housemates' preferences so you can respect them as far as is reasonable.

- Try to ensure you have a quiet space to work.
  - This will usually be your bedroom in student accommodation, but it might also be the library on campus (it might be quieter). You will need to ensure you have space to do your academic work, and you should avoid doing it in the kitchen or other shared areas so that you don't get disturbed, and so others can use that shared space to socialize or relax (remembering that downtime is also important!) without feeling like they are disturbing you. Just remember, if you do work best in the library, ensure you stay safe travelling late at night.

- Communicate with each other.
  - You don't have to be close friends, you don't have to confide in each other, but you do have to live with them (albeit temporarily). Learn to communicate without arguing.

- Only eat the food you have bought.
  - Unless you share the food shop with your flatmates, don't take food that isn't yours.

- Clean up after yourself.
  - This means washing up, tidying up, cleaning the floor. If you are lucky enough to have a cleaner in your Halls of Residence, buy them chocolates once a term as a thank you for clearing up your mess; they are never paid enough to clean up after students!

- Don't bang on people's doors at night unless there's an emergency.

- No loud parties after midnight on weekdays.
  - Yes, you're making memories, but other people are trying to sleep and study. Remember why you are at university, and ensure your priorities are in order. Partying all week is never a priority.

- Try to avoid dangerous practical jokes.
  - When I lived in halls, some of my flatmates played a lot of pranks on us (including a very memorable one with washing-up liquid and a toilet cistern), mostly harmless and entertaining, but I know of other pranks that were not quite so safe. Remember that you should not be putting anyone in harm's way. Have fun, but be safe about it.

- Don't leave your valuables lying around, keep them safe in your room.

- Don't forget your keys.
  - If security keep getting called out to let you into your room, they're going to get quite annoyed.

Dealing with Noise and Disruption

> Be prepared for lots of noise, the doors are heavy, footsteps are heavier.
>
> **Ruby**

Some of the noise and disruption that comes from living in shared student accommodation is unavoidable. You're living with a lot of people in a small space, it will be noisy at times, and it is best to be prepared. Bring headphones and ear plugs for when you need some quiet time. If things get particularly noisy to a level you are unable to manage, try to discuss it politely with your housemates first, if you are comfortable doing so, but if that does not resolve matters, speak to the Accommodation Office and request to move rooms to somewhere quieter.

Sometimes there are particular situations in university accommodation that can be disruptive; for example: excessive targeting of individuals, theft of property and/or food, people banging on windows/doors, or loud music late at night repeatedly despite warnings. For all situations that make living in shared university accommodation disruptive for you, contact the Accommodation Office directly in the day, and Campus Security at night. Put the numbers for both in your phone, and back up your phone calls with emails to confirm any actions that have been agreed.

In university-owned shared student accommodation, you will also find there are regular fire drills. This is a legal requirement and completely necessary. Unfortunately, during the day is no use whatsoever, since most students are supposed to be in classes; you're also awake, meaning that you can move quickly and there's no issue. This means that the best time to test out the fire alarms and everyone's ability to get out of the building quickly is at night, when you may or may not be asleep. What you have to remember is that practising this will keep you safe in the event of a real fire, which is important and could save your life.

Keep a dressing gown or thick jumper by the door, along with your shoes or boots and keys. Roll with it, you will be able to get back to bed before too long. Don't forget to take any guests staying in your room with you: remember, it could be a real fire not a drill.

Private Shared or Rented Accommodation

Celebrate birthdays and other holidays with your flatmates, they become your temporary family.

Sarah

Some students move directly into private accommodation, and some students move into private accommodation after one or more years of study. It is always a good move to live with those we share common interests with, are already friends with, or who have similar preferences for tidiness, sleeping, music, and food. However, we can't always choose these things, so it's beneficial for everyone to be considerate. If you know you like loud music, or you're the only vegan in a group of omnivores, then you need to all communicate about your requirements. Think of it as a list of wishes, and be prepared to negotiate.

Deposits and Letting Fees

> *Always go through the welcome pack and sign off on everything that's there in your room, If you don't, then you'll get charged if it's not there at the end when you move out.*
>
> **Lynn**

Similar to university accommodation, you're bound by rules and regulations in the form of contracts, deposits, and letting fees when you rent a house or flat. The difference with private student accommodation is that not all estate agents and individuals have the same rules. Learning to negotiate these, and work out which is better (hint, cheaper is not always better if you have no legal protection) is a useful skill for when you have to do this post-university, particularly if you're not already familiar with the letting process.

Make sure you read all contracts carefully, check out the insurance your landlord holds and whether you need to get your own. In particular, look at the conditions of your deposit return, and check that your deposit is put into a government-approved tenancy deposit scheme—this is a legal requirement in England and Wales.

Take photographs of the whole house/flat when you move in; if you can record this with your landlord or letting agency, do that too,

209

and keep a record of the fact you've informed them (sending an email and asking for confirmation of receipt is a straightforward way to do this). This way you should be able to clearly resolve any disputes about deposits when you leave. You should also take a meter reading for the fuel and water at this point. You're not responsible for any utilities that are used prior to moving in; again, register this with your landlord or letting agency, and make sure that they clear any outstanding debt left by the previous tenants.

If you are concerned with anything in terms of your new accommodation, you can contact your university Accommodation Office for advice, along with the Students' Union. They can still support you with private accommodation information and support, but you can also contact the Citizens Advice Bureau and they will be able to give you targeted advice that applies to your particular situation. In BOX 9.2, include the key details you need for all those individuals and contacts you will need while you're renting privately.

Most importantly, with shared houses and flats, have fun! This is a brilliant way to live while you're younger, so make sure you embrace

BOX 9.2 Contact Details for Private Rental Accommodation

Contact	Email/Website	Phone Number
Landlord/Letting Agency		
Student Accommodation Office		
Students' Union		
Citizens Advice Bureau	https://www .citizensadvice. org.uk/	See website for local details

the freedom. Stay safe, keep in touch with your housemates, and remember that they will be your family when you're away from home and can often become friends for life, so share all your celebrations and look after each other.

Contribute and Be Respectful of Each Others' Space

> *Bring plug unblocker liquid, your shower drain WILL be blocked with hair and other gross stuff.*
>
> **Sara**

We all hate doing the chores, but it's a necessary part of living independently; if it's something you're not used to, make sure you adapt to doing your fair share. Be respectful of everyone's views and wishes when it comes to shared spaces; we are all different and everyone probably feels just as strongly about what they want. You can be as messy as you like in your own room but don't impose disorder in other rooms of the house if you live with some very tidy people. Similarly, if you have extremely high standards of cleanliness then try to avoid enforcing cleaning rotas/activities on others: discuss and agree an acceptable standard and way forward as a group. Remember, you're also sharing bathrooms and kitchens, and this includes the fridge. Share the cleaning, take your turn taking the bins out, and be mindful of only eating your own food!

It's also important to remember that you will all need to study within your shared accommodation, so ensuring you have your own space to study is important. This will often be your bedroom, as it is most often within university Halls of Residence, but it might also be a communal area designed for study purposes. Try to avoid working in communal rooms so you don't get distracted, and make sure that you respect everyone else's space while they are studying.

Food, Cooking, and Chores

> *Don't be that [person] who leaves the kitchen a mess, tidy up after yourself.*
>
> **Ruby**

You're going to need to buy food and cook when you're living with flatmates. Get yourself a cookbook and start learning if you can't already cook. There are lots of cookbooks and recipe books around, often there are plenty in charity shops. There are also countless recipes available for free, and instantly, online. Make sure you find a book/resource for your level of cooking ability (the student cookbooks tend to assume little to no knowledge of cooking), your food tastes, and your budget.

You should discuss with your housemates if you're doing a group food shop or if you're buying your own individual food. Once you've decided this, make sure you set your weekly budget for spending on food, then go to shops that allow you to maximize your budget. Try to avoid your local convenience store (prices tend to be higher), and do bulk shops once a week, or once a fortnight, at the nearest supermarket (most have online shopping available). If you share the food shop as a household, make sure you stick to a list and ensure that everyone's needs are accommodated.

Once you're settled into your new accommodation it's often a good idea to set up a rota for chores and evening meals (if you want to cook as a household). A rota is useful as it helps share the chores, enables you to share your food tastes with your flatmates, and also share the washing up afterwards! As noted earlier though, try not to enforce a rota on everyone but create one as a household (if possible)—that way everyone is hopefully bought into the idea. I've given you an example in BOX 9.3 but adapt this as needed if it's something that will work

BOX 9.3 The Household Rota

Chores	Frequency	Person
Washing up	Daily	
Cleaning the bathroom	Weekly	
Cleaning the kitchen	Weekly	
Taking the bins out	Weekly	
Hoovering	Weekly	
Cooking	Weekly	

for you. The idea is to set out a sensible schedule for everything that needs doing in the place you live, but work it around busy periods in everyone's lives. Crucially though, you should divide and conquer, don't leave it all to someone else and assume it will just get done.

Resolving Disputes

Make a cleaning rota.

Kallie

One thing that is guaranteed to happen at some point, whatever your living situation, is a difference of opinion between you and your housemates/family. House meetings are an important part of living with adults, they are a great way to discuss and resolve issues and differences of opinion. Learning to compromise is a key part of living with other adults, because not everything will always be perfectly as

213

you wish it to be. Sometimes you will need to take part in difficult conversations, but they are part and parcel of working and living with other adults. It's always useful to set up some guidelines early on that you all agree with and are happy to stick to when you are having house meetings. It is useful to remember that not all disputes will be completely resolved to everyone's satisfaction. Discussion can make things easier, but sometimes you will need to agree to disagree in the interests of home harmony.

Discussing any issues as they arise might prevent disagreements and help you avoid long-term mutual disrespect and disharmony; it definitely makes for a better living experience even if it's not always comfortable to discuss some issues that come up. You don't want anyone storing up resentments and then have these explode later on into arguments—that can lead to a very negative living experience. This applies to those of you living with parent/s, caregiver/s, and your own family as well, so it's something to keep in mind for all kinds of living arrangements.

Living at Home with Parents/ Caregivers: Finding Your Own Space

> You have to respect that you're living in your parents' home, but they have to respect that you're studying at the same time, and there has to be a consensus on 'how's this going to work'.
>
> **Alice**

I've used the terms family, parent/s, and caregiver/s in this section, but I'm aware there are myriad personal circumstances that are very different to the perception of a typical family. This section is for those of you who will live in the same residence you grew up in, with the adults who raised you.

There are an increasing number of students living in their child-hood homes during their degrees, either by choice or by necessity. University studies are more expensive than ever, and with increasing living costs it can make financial sense for many students to live with their families during their studies.

However, if this applies to you, that doesn't mean you should carry on letting them look after you! There will be times where you want to go out with your friends, and not be held to the same curfews that you may have had while at school. But equally, there will also be times when your family need you to be the responsible adult you now are and look after younger siblings, other family members, take the dog for a walk, or be in when someone is making a delivery.

Once you start your degree, you should sit down and have a meeting with your family; discuss a new format for what is, and is not, acceptable to all of you. Bring your timetable and travel needs with you, so that you can make sure your family is fully informed. While you're at university you're growing into a more independent and fuller version of yourself. This is your time to learn to be really independent, but you can't do this if you're still taking on the role of a teenager. Make sure that you keep communication open and honest, but also respectful, while you're living at home.

─────── VANESSA'S TOP TIPS ───────
for living with family

> Compartmentalizing your home situation makes for a much less stressful home life.
>
> **Cassie**

- Discuss your commute and share your university timetable.
  - Particularly useful if you need to borrow the car and/or need to make sure you are free of family commitments on particular days.
- Do your own laundry.
  - Your family will be eternally grateful. Remember to ask if you don't already know how to use the washing machine.
- Join in the cooking rota.
  - If you can't already, learn to cook and give your family the night off sometimes.
- Contribute to the household bills!
  - Your maintenance loan is not just for books and drinking. You could do the food shop once a fortnight, or give your parent/s or caregiver/s some money each term to help cover the costs of you still living there.
- Take your turn cleaning.
  - Run the hoover round every so often and clean the bathroom every few weeks. Your family will appreciate this, and it will buy you goodwill if you end up staying out really late some nights.
- Don't bring other people back home with you after a night out.
  - This is a family home and you cannot treat it like a university Hall of Residence. Maintain respect and don't cross those boundaries. This means no house parties and no partners overnight without express permission.

Studying at Home

> A space to work uninterrupted—talk to your household so they understand how important it is for you to be able to work undisturbed, this may include telling them that 'no biscuits in the cupboard or their sister hogging the remote' do not constitute emergencies. Put a note on the closed door, if necessary, to remind them!
>
> **Nicky**

Finding your own space is just as important when you're living at home. If you don't have your own room then you need to find a space that is just yours where you can study undisturbed, this will be really important for your concentration and learning.

Not all parents/caregivers will understand how much work goes into doing a degree; there are many students each year who are known as 'first-generation' students who are the first in their families to go to university. Obviously, this is a wonderful thing, but it can be a confusing and stressful time when families don't understand what is involved and there are conflicts between expectations and reality.

Giving them this book to read will help, but make sure they understand how often you will need space to work, and what your degree involves. Share your timetable and explain that you have to do a lot of work outside of classes as well.

Crucially, when living at home, be honest and open in your communications and ask that they be the same. If your socializing is impacting the household, they need to let you know and you need to be responsive to this. Have a discussion around boundaries and mutual guidelines for behaviour; if you set up ground rules for what to expect early on, you can avoid a lot of conflict later on.

Living with Your Own Family: Finding Your Own Space and Time

> Personally, with children, I would advise hiding in a cupboard so they don't find you studying or writing essays. Seriously though, it is essential to get a rota in place for your own sanity so you have a balance between uni work/work/family and home commitments.
> **Michelle**

I've mentioned that life often involves juggling a lot of roles and situations (see Chapter 9), and families are a significant consideration for an increasing number of students; many students now attend university after having had their own families. It's not as easy to organize your learning around a demanding group of younger people that you are responsible for and whom you need to prioritize over your studies. It is possible to juggle raising children and studying, and many have done so in the past, but it does require an extra level of thought, consideration, and organization; this means rotas, calendars, and creating 'zones' with your time.

A useful thing to do is to explain to your children, and partner if you have one, what studying at university entails, and the benefits for you all once you get your degree. Children are remarkably adaptable, but some age groups can be more challenging than others, particularly if they are used to getting your undivided attention or have additional support needs themselves. If your partner, or family support unit, didn't go to university, make sure they understand the commitment you need to give your degree, and make sure they're onside and happy to help you juggle the various challenges you need to face as a family.

Talk through, as a family, what you need in order to complete your studies, and ask them to let you know what you can do to make it easier for them. Setting out clear boundaries and expectations early on will make for a much smoother transition to studying. It will also help to have a reliable childminder, or supportive relative/friend, on hand as well if you are able to put that in place.

One thing that will help, particularly if you have children, is having your own space to study—ideally that won't be your bedroom, although sometimes this is unavoidable. Creating your own (relatively) private study space will be incredibly useful, both for ensuring that there's a clear and demonstrable boundary around the space where your family knows you're not to be disturbed, and also so that you have a clear space that you can mentally associate with work. Just make sure it's off limits to your children, unless they have your permission—that way you know things won't be moved when you get back to your study periods.

Compartmentalizing your life into 'zones' is a really useful exercise, for working parents as well as parents who are focused on their studies full time. Create space within the week for your studies, for household chores, for family time, and all the things you need to fit in.

Finding Family Time

> There has to be a balance or you will start to struggle by letting things get on top of you. You will have gaps in between lectures, use those to study and read so that at weekends you're able to spend time with your family.
>
> *Emma*

Juggling the different strands of your family life can get mildly chaotic at time (see Chapter 9). Spending time together as a family is incredibly important and will help all of you remain a close-knit unit while you are committed to your studies. Decide as a family on a day in the week (or an afternoon, or even a couple of evenings a week) you can all spend together, and then stick to this as far as you can.

For certain times of the year, it might be more difficult to stick to this regular family time; you might have extra work on, for example during exam season or when you have lots of deadlines. Make sure you arrange something special for when you have time, that way your family knows that they will spend some time with you, and it makes it easier to get that bit of space you need to complete your studies. It doesn't have to be going out or spending lots of money, it just needs to be something you can enjoy together. You could watch a movie or you could head out for a weekend adventure, for example heading to a local park, forest, or a local visitor attraction; something that everyone will enjoy.

In BOX 9.4 there is a 'Negotiation' list. This is where you can put down all the things together that will come up, and what compensation is going to happen for that particular busy situation. This can be for your family members as well as for you, so that everyone gets involved.

BOX 9.4 The Negotiation List

Situation	Compensation	Day of Compensation
Example: Needing to work on an assignment the week of a deadline	*Movie Night with kids (including special popcorn: aka popcorn with sweets and chocolates mixed in)*	*Friday night 6 p.m.*
Example: Needing to revise for exams	*Weekend outdoor adventure (e.g. Hadrian's Wall)*	*The first weekend after exams*

Ultimately, when you live with your family, it's likely to resemble mild chaos for much of the time, and this will only become more pronounced while you're studying on top of everything else. Accept that things will be messy, the house will not always be clean, and that sometimes the children will watch too much TV. You can't do everything for everyone, so during your studies (and indeed generally) decide what is really important to you; don't worry about the rest; relax and embrace the chaos.

Moving Home during Your Degree

I moved a few times, I planned it around uni breaks
Jake

While you'll ideally have a secure base during your studies, it is often the case that students move around quite a lot during their degrees. For those who don't own their own homes, university life is often characterized by frequent moving between residences; this might be between university halls and your family home, or it might be between multiple student houses. Planning is a necessary part of any house move, but it's doubly so if you're moving while studying.

Studying at university isn't like a job, you can't just take a few days off to move house when you have classes to get to, because those classes aren't repeated and you will miss out on crucial information that you need for your studies and assignments.

If you can, plan moves for outside of term time. If you're not able to and moving in term time is necessary then contact your tutors and let them know what is happening; ask them how you can catch up with the work afterwards. Don't simply be absent without letting them know why you're not there. They will understand things like a house move can't be helped, but it is always polite to let them know.

Moving Back in with Your Parent/s or Caregiver/s

> *Going from halls to living at home was a really big change, because you develop your own way of doing things.*
>
> **Sarah**

Sometimes, for many reasons, you might have to move out of student-style accommodation and back home with your parent/s or caregiver/s, and this can be a big change. Living at home is very different from living in university accommodation, and you'll need to make sure you sit down with your family and discuss how you're going to make it work.

It won't be the same as when you were growing up. Technically you've now left home and are returning; you're an independent adult moving back home and it's now a qualitatively different situation compared to when you were younger. You may have developed particular routines, and now need to consider what time you're having a shower or playing music late at night. Be prepared to have to compromise and negotiate a new format to your living arrangements. Reading the section above on living with your parents/caregivers will certainly help with this. But crucially, be patient. There will be a period of adjustment, but hopefully this will be short-lived.

When Accommodation Options Are a Challenge

> *Family life is a tough topic for some of us . . . this is a chance to break away from it for a while and see if you're ready to thrive on your own. For some of you this will be a very affirmative and life changing decision.*
>
> **Adam S**

It's important to remember that not everyone has a smooth journey when it comes to accommodation. Sometimes we have students being evicted, sometimes students end up getting kicked out of the family home, and sometimes they end up sofa-surfing with friends because they either can't afford, or don't have, a place of their own, so they end up homeless.

If you fall into the category of student who has any accomodation challenges, either when you start or during your studies, you need to contact your key programme contacts, as well as the student accommodation team at your university. Chapters 2 and 13 have information on finances and getting extra support, and you should always contact your Personal Tutor and University Support Services to let them know your situation. There are many areas where people can help you, and making sure you know who to turn to when you have challenges is really important. Crucially though, don't ever feel embarrassed; don't worry what anyone will think; simply get in touch with the people in BOX 9.5, and get the support you need.

BOX 9.5 Contacts for Accommodation Support

Contact	Contact details
Programme Leader	
Personal Tutor	
Another Lecturer/Tutor I trust	
Student Accomodation Office	
Students' Union	
Citizens Advice Bureau	https://www.citizensadvice.org.uk/ See website for local details
Unviersity Finance team	
University Well-being/Support Service	

A Final Word

> Let go! Accept that sometimes . . . probably most of the time . . . your house [or flat] will be a mess! You will always have a pile of ironing! Your garden will be weedy! You can't do everything so decide what is really important to you and let go of the rest . . . it doesn't really matter.
>
> **Nicky**

Students have many different types of living arrangement; all come with their challenges and considerations. Be aware of the potential challenges, show willingness to compromise and negotiate, and your living situation will be a much more pleasant experience. If you need support with accommodation, or you find yourself without acommodation altogether, don't forget your university can help you—all you need to do is ask.

www.oup.com/he/parson1e

Visit the online resources where you will find additional materials including guides on time management, financial planning and budgeting, mindfulness and mental health, hints and tips, as well as all the tables from the book.

Chapter 10

RELATIONSHIPS
AND BOUNDARIES

Why This Chapter Is Important

- Forming healthy relationships with your fellow students and staff at university is an important part of your academic journey and provides a sense of belonging that will prove a key factor in your academic journey. This chapter looks at different types of relationships, and how to successfully navigate them.

- Sometimes relationships take a darker turn. When this happens you need to know how to both tackle this and where to report it, if necessary. This chapter goes through some of the ways you can help keep yourself safe on, and off, campus, and who to turn to if things go wrong.

> *Some people do genuinely want a little bit of help . . . others are going to be people who just try to be friends with you because they want to get a better grade.*
>
> **Alice**

When you come to university you meet a lot of new people, but of course you already have people in your lives that you have existing relationships with. This chapter will cover maintaining and developing relationships with others, and will look at platonic, familial, romantic, and professional relationships. We will also cover some of the negative situations which students can potentially find themselves in, such as unhealthy relationships and relationship breakdowns. We understand that you don't study in an academic vacuum, so your life will impact your studies. As I've mentioned before, Chapter 13 has all the core sources of support for when something goes wrong.

Relationships are important to all of us, they make us feel like we belong to a group and can provide us with a sense of safety and security. Forming new relationships with people you meet at university is vital for your sense of belonging and well-being. While these typically form in the offline world, they can be formed in the online world too. As any gamers will know, it is possible to make friends with people online just as easily as we can in the classroom or the pub. These online friendships and potentially romantic relationships are just as solid and strong as those formed offline, so this is still something you can develop while you're at university, regardless of the type of degree you do.

Making New Friends

> Know your own self-worth . . . you need to be with people who are going to motivate and inspire you, you need to be with people who are like minded.
>
> **Alice**

Some of the friendships you make at university will last a lifetime. Some of my most important friendships were formed at university, and my life is certainly all the better for meeting these individuals. I see the rollercoaster development of student friendships every year; new friendships are formed, dramas occur, friendship groups shift, and some friendships are left by the wayside; occasionally friendships turn into relationships, which come with their own set of situations for students to negotiate.

You'll mix with a lot of new people during university, and while this is wonderful for broadening your horizons and opening up your world to new opportunities, it can feel quite intimidating for some students. For some of you, friendships might form outside your course group, through societies, sports groups, or simply meeting other people around campus (see Chapter 5) and taking option modules outside your subject area (see Chapter 4).

I mentioned back in Chapter 5 that most students are nervous during the early days at university, so this is something you need to keep in mind when you're in your classes and interacting with others on your course and around campus: you're very much not alone. Everyone comes to university with a predefined set of expectations, and their own set of experiences with friendships, which get rapidly adjusted by the reality of the university experience. Join in with activities, conversations, and classes, and you will be on the right path to feeling like part of the university community.

Most students will be fine with a hesitant 'Hi' to start a conversation, some may even be very confident about talking to new people. If you're a mature student you will have had more practice here, even if you're on the shy side, so if you see a young, very shy student sitting alone, do make sure you go and say hello. The reverse applies if you're a student coming straight from school or college and are really nervous about talking to other people; make sure you go and say hello to a mature student. You might not form a lasting friendship, but knowing there is someone in class you can talk to and become 'uni' friends with is really important for your sense of belonging while you're at university.

The key thing to remember is that you are at university to do a degree; you do not need to live in each other's pockets or classes. There are occasional reasons to move to the same classes, for example you might car share to get to university, but you should never move classes just to be with your friends. It might also be the case that your friends are not on your course, so you need to learn to work with your peers studying alongside you. Treat classes as education and a chance to interact with other people; practise the skill of communicating with your peers. After all, you'll be working with a lot of people after university, and you won't be friends with them all, but you will still need to learn how to work with them; university is a great place to practise this. Just remember, negative inter-peer behaviours can feel quite disruptive and result in students not attending class. It's important to keep in mind that all of your classmates are coming to university with different perceptions and experiences; be respectful and polite, but also, don't allow others to dictate your responses or behaviours. If you see any behaviour that is negatively impacting you or others in your class that you yourself are unable to handle, be sure to mention it to your tutors and ask for support.

When Love and Romance Blossom at University

> If you are still together by the time you finish uni, then he/she is definitely a keeper!
>
> SB

Sometimes, friendship turns into something more at university. This can be a wonderful thing, and I've heard many stories from starry-eyed students saying how glad they are they came to the university because if they hadn't, they wouldn't have met their partners.

I'm absolutely not going to give out any relationship advice here, but what I am going to say is to make sure your relationship doesn't impact on your academic life. I've seen students joined at the hip; I've seen students sleeping on each other's shoulders during lectures, relying on the other to make their notes; and I've seen students who have arguments in the middle of the corridor between classes, and others who just gaze at each other in class while completely ignoring the tutor. All of these are things that should ideally *not* happen as they are disruptive to your education. You don't need to be joined at the hip; in fact it's far healthier if you're not always together and are able to navigate your other friendships alongside your relationship. Plus, you should take responsibility for your own learning and stay awake in class!

It really is lovely when relationships form, and you should enjoy the heightened sense of well-being this gives you while they last. Just make sure you focus on your studies when you're in class, and not on each other (and keep your fights private)!

Maintaining Friendships Outside University

> It's difficult to manage, depending on what they're doing. If they're doing a degree, they understand, which is really helpful.
>
> **Alice**

When you get to university, it's easy to get swept up in the new exciting environment you're now a part of. Sometimes your friends back

229

home can feel a bit left out, particularly if they're not going through the same university experience.

For most people it's important to make sure that you don't leave existing friends behind while you're blazing trails towards your degree and future career. These are the friends who know you best; they grew up with you and may even know you better than your own families, so their support is invaluable. Finding time to connect on a regular basis is really important.

Social media is a great tool, but it's not the same as picking up the phone, video calling, messaging regularly, going for coffee, or having a night out. Spending real non-social media time with your existing friends is as important as making new friends while you're at univeristy. This is particularly important if you're an international student and/or have travelled across country to attend university; hearing each others' voices and seeing each others' faces is an effective tool to sustain friendships. Regular messages are great, but schedule that phone or video call to really make sure your friendship doesn't suffer during your studies.

One thing that is great for maintaining bonds across distance and differing experiences is humour. Sharing the latest meme, or having a giggle over something you all find funny will maintain the bonds between you. Everyone is busy, but even sharing brief messages and funny pictures can help keep that close bond going while you're apart.

However, it is important to add a note that not everyone has a close group of friends outside of university. Sometimes university is an escape route from difficult personal circumstances, and a chance to reinvent yourself and create a better future. There are many reasons why this might be the case, and if this is the case for you, embrace the new experience but make sure you keep in touch with those people in your pre-university life that have supported you until this point, if you are lucky enough to have them. But remember, going to university provides you with a wealth of new opportunities, so regardless of your personal situation, making new friends and maintaining existing bonds will enhance that experience.

Looking After The Bonds with Your Significant Others

> *Maintain a healthy balance! Make time to see your family and friends and your significant other around your university schedule. When things get harder at uni (exam season, deadlines, and dissertation), they will be your biggest support system so try to hold on to them. Yes, your degree is important—but so are your relationships!*
>
> **Taylor**

The demographic spread of students attending university is widening all the time, so more students than ever have family members and significant others that they need to look after and/or maintain relationships with. In addition, with the rising cost of a university education and the cost of living, a significant proportion of UK students are increasingly living at home for the duration of their degrees. Where you live is a subject for Chapter 9, but when you live with family members or significant others, it's important to have a clear line of communication between you, particularly if you are the first person to do a degree in your family.

Often, when students come from families where few others have degrees, it can be difficult to communicate with them exactly how university works and what you need. My top tip here would obviously be to get them to read this book! But you should also communicate clearly about your workload and what you need from them in order to feel supported in your studies. Keeping that communication open throughout your degree is really important for a healthy relationship with your family and significant others.

It's particularly challenging if you have children who need your time and attention as they don't always understand the demands your studies make on you. Finding time to spend with each other is important, but you should also make sure that you don't give yourself a hard time for studying a lot. You're working at this degree for them as much as for yourself; the degree you eventually get will hopefully lead to job opportunities and a better life for them and they will understand in time. Weekends are a great time to make sure you get some quality time together, even just having a movie or games night once a week can be a big deal to children (and it's probably not a bad idea for you too!).

Maintaining Your Relationships

> Always make time for your loved ones, they're there to help you and want the best for you. Don't push them away.
>
> **Rhiannon**

When you're in a relationship, be that platonic friendship, familial, or romantic, it's necessary to accept that everyone is different and it's not possible to read each other's minds. Accepting these differences and respecting boundaries are key factors in maintaining relationships.

All relationships take time to develop, so stay positive and make time for the people you enjoy being around. As long as you communicate clearly and honestly, the relationships will develop in a healthy manner, whichever direction they develop in. And if a relationship does dwindle until one, or both, of you lose interest, make sure you accept that change is a part of life and try not to be too upset for long. Yes, some relationships take longer to recover from, but you will still recover from it. As my mum says, 'this too shall pass'; it's good advice, so keep it in mind.

─────── **VANESSA'S TOP TIPS** ───────

for maintaining relationships with others

> Look after your friends, check that they're OK.
> **Kathy**

- Make time to connect and catch up.

- Respect each other's boundaries.

- Pay attention to them.

- Think about how the things you say might impact them or make them feel.

- Listen to understand what is being said, don't just listen to reply.

- Make sure you allow time for space from the relationship as well.

- Trust in each other.

- If conflict arises, try to remain calm and objective, and be thoughtful when resolving it.

- Have their back when others are speaking about them.

- Be honest.

The Dark Side of Relationships (and How to Get Support if You're Affected)

> You can really trick yourself into thinking things are alright, even though you know they're not, so just be honest with yourself.
> **Sarah**

The friendships you form in your early weeks will quickly feel irreplaceable, but this doesn't mean they are immune to the challenges all relationships face. If you feel that you've outgrown a friendship, usually the lack of contact and emotional distance means the connection fizzles out of its own accord. However, sometimes there are disagreements and a conflict of viewpoint or opinion that can't be resolved. If this conflict impacts your classes it can be very disruptive for you and everyone else in the class. But it can also have a significant impact on your mental health.

What you need to do is remember that university, fun as it can be at times, is a professional environment. Save the conflict for outside of class. If you are trying to do this, but another student will not 'let it go' during class, then you can speak to one of your tutors and/or lecturers. Anything that disrupts class we can deal with, and if it needs to be resolved through more formal channels, we can help you do this as well. If there is a deeper-seated issue that can't be resolved, or is potentially only impacting you and not others in your class, you should speak to the Student Support Team, or contact one of the external support services listed in Chapter 13.

When Relationships Take a Sinister Turn

> The mental health support at the university is very good and the staff are very understanding. You just have to talk to them.
>
> **Nickayla**

Sometimes what seems to be a friendship or romantic relationship can turn into something that is one-sided and has an element of negativity about it. Bullying, gender-based violence, exclusion from social groups, or any other breakdown of the relationship can cause emotional distress and impact you personally and academically. This is something we understand and there is support for this within universities, so is not something to just handle alone.

If someone you have become close to is doing any of the following, you need to take steps to ensure that you can safely remove yourself from that relationship. If you aren't sure how to do this, or are feeling intimidated by the person you're involved with, always talk to a member of staff.

—————————— **VANESSA'S TOP TIPS** ——————————
for RED FLAGS to look out for in the behaviour of others

> If you have a good rapport with a lecturer, just go and tell them what's going on.
>
> **Milo**

- Always appearing where you are.
- Responding negatively to messages.
- Expecting you to drop everything for them.
- Always expecting you to be the one making time for them, and always on their terms.
- Saying negative things about you behind your back.
- Saying negative things about you to others when you are present.
- Dismissing your views and ignoring your feelings.
- Commenting negatively about your other relationships.
- Wanting you to always share your work.
  - (Never do this to even your closest friends and partners!)
  - This is academic misconduct (see Chapter 6), and anyone who cares about you will never want you to get into trouble for this.
- Making fun of you, your beliefs, practices, actions, and/or feelings.
- Not allowing you to make decisions for yourself, or making you afraid to do so.

- Threatening you or making you feel threatened.

- Embarrassing you and/or putting you down (privately or publicly).

- Manipulating or controlling you.

- Disrespecting your sexual orientation and preferences.

- Making you feel like you don't have any personal space.

- Isolating you from others you care about.

- Behaving in a way that makes you feel nauseated and/or anxious when they are unhappy or irritated.

If any of these red flags start appearing, and it is connected with someone on campus or in your classes, make sure you go and speak to the people you've listed in BOX 10.1. But you should also speak to the teams of staff in place to support you; see Chapter 13 for this, as well as BOX 10.1.

BOX 10.1 Policies and Complaints Procedures

Source/Policy	Where to Find Them/It (Plus Contact Numbers and Emails)
Programme Leader	
Personal Tutor	
Another Lecturer I trust	
Students Union	
Support Services/Well-being	
Campus Police	
Complaints Policy	
Professional Standards Policy	
Student Handbook	

If it's happening with someone off campus, then you need the support teams and possibly some outside help. On campus you can find the people in BOX 10.1, and off campus, there is a list of support services you can access in Chapter 13. Most importantly, talk to someone and get some support; you will probably be surprised by how many people understand exactly what you're going through.

Online Interference and Finding Room to Breathe

> People would discuss assignments and how they had already finished, etc. Which used to set my anxiety off, as I'd be sitting there thinking I must not know/understand if I still couldn't complete the assignment. . .So, I had to learn when essays were due to avoid those conversations. This meant balancing feeling rude for not being social with not putting myself in a situation that could lead to a panic attack.
>
> **Kay**

Everyone needs space to breathe; whether it's a hot bubble bath or a couple of hours playing a favourite game or sport, finding space to think and relax by ourselves is really important. Social media is a big part of most students' lives now, and students can be super-connected in a way that used to not be the case. Prior to social media, the home might have been considered a safe space where recovery from arguments and disagreements could happen. Now, with social media and messaging, there is no room to breathe in friendships, and that's actually not very healthy psychologically.

The online sphere is not immune from negative behaviours that cause concerns: cyberbullying and creeping (which can lead to cyberstalking) are an increasing concern, despite legislation attempting to protect online users from these behaviours. If you, or someone you know, is subject to any behaviours that can be construed as cyberbullying and/or cyberstalking, you should use BOX 10.1 to report it.

If you need some space from a friend, consider turning your phone off, or ignoring your social media for a while. If your friendship is becoming more confrontational than you'd like, and you feel that you do not need to be connected to that person anymore, my top tip is to remove them from your social media apps. If there are overt actions directed at you that are impacting your studies, you should contact either Student Support Services or any of the staff listed in BOX 10.1.

The most important thing to remember is that anyone who cares about you will understand the need for personal space. If they don't understand, or it creates tension and disagreement, then it is perhaps time to move that particular friendship into a more professional format. Again, if there are difficulties here, contact any of the staff listed on this page, but Student Support Services and your Personal Tutor are great places to start.

Advice for Families and Significant Others

Get parents to read this book.
Sarah

The main advice for your parents and significant others is to read this book (where they are old enough to do so). This way they will be able to understand your journey at university and the support and options available to you.

We take privacy of our students seriously. Due to national privacy regulations, we are unable to communicate with outside individuals without student permission. Indeed, we are not even allowed to confirm if an individual is a student at the university, for their own protection. If you are connected with a university student and have some concerns about relationships they are involved in, or their behaviours and health in general, then the first step is obviously to communicate with them and encourage them to follow the support options available to them, listed in all chapters but predominantly in this chapter and Chapter 13.

Often prompting students to ask for support is enough, but where you do have additional concerns and wish to communicate with the university directly, you will need to ask the student you are connected with to grant us permission for you to communicate. This can be as simple as an email from the student, telling us that we have permission to speak with you about them. Once this permission is granted, we can communicate with you directly and support you in resolving any difficulties that arise.

Developing a Professional Relationship with Staff (and How to Maintain Boundaries during Your Degree)

> Be polite. Don't treat email like an instant messenger or texting function. Remember they have work to do and lives to live too, and you aren't the only person they need to get to. You aren't entitled to immediate and in-depth response from ANYONE, let alone your lecturers, and this is something you need to learn for life as well as academia.
>
> Sol

Just like people in all walks of life, academics are a varied group of people with individual personalities and attitudes towards teaching, learning, and interacting. As you get to know your lecturers, you will come to understand that while there is a wide variety of approaches, everyone is there to support you and help you towards your goal of getting a degree.

You will, however, need to respect your lecturers' and tutors' time and space. All unviersity staff have lives outside campus, they will have families to take care of and friends to spend time with, so you cannot expect them to be available 24/7. If you email after 5 p.m., before 9 a.m., or over the weekend, be prepared to wait for a reply. Standard email reply times are set at between 48 and 72 hours to account for staff having home lives and busy teaching schedules. So please keep this in mind before you rattle off several emails to your lecturers or tutors.

Annual leave is another time period when you need to be respectful of staff boundaries. All academics should have an automatic 'out of office' email reply set up during annual leave, which should tell you when they are back at work. After this date, you can usually expect a response in 24–48 hours. This is one of the reasons why using your unversity email is the best option for communicating with staff; most other messaging systems and VLEs do not have an 'out of office' option, so we cannot alert you to our absence.

VANESSA'S TOP TIPS

for interacting with university staff

Strictly no text talk!
SB

- Introduce yourself if you have only recently met.
  - Don't be offended if they ask your name!
- Be polite and respectful at all times.
- If you need to see them in person, try to stick to their office hours.
  - Sometimes called Student Hours or 'Drop-In' sessions.
- Don't be over-friendly and maintain a professional distance.
  - Even if you see them out in the pubs and clubs, be polite, but don't join them in a social situation.

- – Don't befriend them on personalized social media such as Facebook and Snapchat.
- – Don't swap phone numbers.
- If you do need to confide in them, keep in mind it is a professional conversation, and they will remain objective while they are being supportive during your discussion.
- Be patient when waiting for email replies.
  - – Remember your lecturers are busy people and an instant response is rarely possible.
  - – Email is not instant messenger, it is a formal letter delivery system.
- Don't overstep professional boundaries.
  - – You're going to come into contact with many academics (your lecturers and tutors) during your degree, and some of them you will get on really well with. That's fantastic, and it is lovely when this happens. However, you do need to remember that there are some boundaries that cannot be crossed. No matter how friendly we are, you (and we) should remain professional at all times. If your relationship develops from professional to personal, and on rare occasions this can legitimately happen, then it can wait until after you have graduated to pursue it.

So, when you're emailing staff at the university, keep it professional and be polite. Don't link up with them on the more personal social media sites (e.g. Facebook and SnapChat) and don't exchange phone numbers for any reason, including WhatsApp. Save anything that is indicative of a friendship for after you graduate.

Staff–Student Connection/Interaction Issues

If they talk down to you, that says more of them than it does of you
Alice

Hopefully your interactions with staff will be professional and supportive; however, it would be remiss of me not to cover the situations where this isn't the case. Sometimes individuals can cross professional boundaries and this can lead to distress for the student or staff member, along with others involved in the situation. There are many scenarios where this might happen: a staff member may pursue a relationship with a student (with or without permission) or vice versa; there might be negative attitudes surrounding a particular set of individuals; students can be abusive towards staff; or there might be some more sinister elements that cross professional, ethical, and moral boundaries.

All situations which cross professional boundaries should be reported to someone within your department, ideally your Personal Tutor or your Programme Leader. You can also seek out Support Services and the Students' Union for advice and guidance. Whoever you are able to turn to will be able to discuss the procedures and policies that exist, and will be able to help you with potential complaints and the resulting impact.

If you do become involved in a negative situation of any kind, you should check out what policies exist within your university and the procedure for putting in a complaint. Hopefully you will never need this, but just in case, complete the checklist in BOX 10.1 so that you have the information to hand.

A Final Word

> *Some of you will miss your families a great deal. . .remember you aren't alone. University is an excellent chance to make new and different friends of all ages from all walks of life, and a new surrogate family is there for you to find.*
>
> *Adam S*

Relationships are vital for our well-being and making sure you find time to maintain your relationships with the people you care about is as important as making new friends on your course. No matter what kind of relationships you're coming to university with, you will hopefully leave with plenty more friendships than when you started that will potentially be with you, supporting you, for life. Finally, while it's always great when staff and students get on well, do make sure you maintain professional boundaries during your degree.

www.oup.com/he/parson1e

Visit the online resources where you will find additional materials including guides on time management, financial planning and budgeting, mindfulness and mental health, hints and tips, as well as all the tables from the book.

Resources

'The Mix—essential support for the under 25s' (https://www.themix.org.uk) has a great set of resources for all things connected with gender, mental health, sexuality, and relationships, as well as much more. There is also crisis support available through this site.

Chapter 11

SOCIALIZING AND STAYING SAFE

Why This Chapter Is Important

- One of the things everybody associates with university is the social life. While widening participation means a change in student demographic, social events are still a feature of your university years. This chapter takes you through the key considerations for socializing, including finding a balance with your studies.

- Not all social experiences are positive, and it's important to stay safe. This chapter goes through some sensible tips as well as looking at what to do when social situations go awry.

> *Socializing is a great way to blow off steam and let your hair down and relax, but if you do this every weekend it can become an issue so keep it to a minimum.*
>
> **Callum**

Socializing is one of the things that almost everyone associates with university: parties, clubbing, drinking, and so forth. While it's great to embrace the social side of university, it is vital to remember that this is not *why* you're going to university. In my first ever lecture at university, the lecturer told me that university is 50% getting a degree, and 50% learning to be an independent adult. According to the data for 2020/21 (HESA, 2022), over a million students live away from home during university, and around 900,000 students live with parents/guardians or in their own home. This means that the historical image of 'young students living away from home' simply does not apply, and student backgrounds and priorities are more varied than ever. In a world where university fees apply, there must be a corresponding shift in focus and a corresponding shift in priorities to account for all student backgrounds, priorities, and demographics.

The image of socializing at university stereotypically includes alcohol, often in excessive quantities, but this is not always the case now. While some students do conform to this stereotype, now many students have jobs, have families, live at home, and may prefer not to drink at all when they do socialize. In addition, some cultures and faiths do not permit drinking alcohol, and many students simply prefer not to for health reasons. I didn't drink alcohol during either of my degrees; I'm well aware that alcohol is not necessary for a fun night out. It is very important to respect your fellow students' views around socialization choices and avoid pressuring others into making decisions they are not comfortable with.

Embrace the social side of university, but make sure it is within some sensible limits and you stay safe. This chapter will focus on how to balance socializing and studying, including how to deal with the after-effects of a particularly heavy night out when you need to get to class. I have also included a section about what to do when something goes wrong while you're socializing on- or off-campus, including abuse of all forms. If this is a section that will be triggering for you in any way, please do feel free to skip it completely.

Finding Your Balance and Making Sure Your Priorities Work for You

> *Socializing is important; no-one expects you to go to uni and not have a life but when partying takes over then we need to look at priorities. My best advice is, if you want a great weekend then work hard during the week so you have no work to do over the weekend. It's all about balance.*
>
> **Aleem**

You, in common with most students, will likely need to juggle lots of different roles while you're a student: employee, partner, parent, friend, member of a community, and so on. As we covered in Chapter 8, you will need to juggle different parts of your life and work hard on your time management and organizational skills. However, what may come as a surprise to many of you is that there are a large number of students who forget to add in a social element to their university journey, meaning they are at risk of feeling adrift, alone, and unsupported during their studies. They are also, crucially, at risk of burning out, which means they may not reach their potential and are more likely to develop mental health difficulties or experience worsening of existing mental health issues.

Making sure you incorporate a social element to your studies is important to promote good mental health, a sense of engagement and inclusion, and a necessary element of stress relief that can support you in your studies throughout your time at university. Some students find it very easy to find social opportunities, while others prefer to look to the Student Union for more organized, and often free, events (see Chapter 5).

All students will have their own socialization preferences and experiences. Some students enjoy the noise of clubs and pubs, but some students will prefer a quieter socialization experience, so consideration of personal preferences and approaches to socializing in an inclusive manner is important.

You may find that many of your peers want to party all the time, and they want you to join them. Make sure you remember why you are at university: you're there to get a degree. If you need to get some work done, or you just want some space and quiet, then you should say no and focus on what you need to focus on.

Sometimes, there are financial considerations around socializing: you might need to save your money for selected nights out, or you might experience financial poverty and have to prioritize your funds for more important things such as food. Chapter 3 covers financial support and advice, but it is helpful to be mindful and accepting of the fact that students arrive at university with very different financial situations, so avoid making assumptions about what others can afford.

The trick is not to socialize so much that your studies become secondary and relegated further down your priority list. You want to make sure you get some work done *before* you go out. You don't have to become regimented with this, as strict deadlines may only add pressure; rather, you want to ensure you have balance and flexibility in your schedule so that you can adapt to social events as they arise and are able to complete your studies effectively around them.

It can be lots of fun, getting swept up in the social life at university. I do remember how tempting it is to head to the pub every night and go clubbing several times a week. But degrees now are very different from when I was a student. Now there are university fees, the need for additional employment, and a significantly increased number of students with families to look after. Students now need to ensure they have a life balance in favour of responsibility, with fun squeezed in where there is time.

Staying Safe When out Having Fun

> Always go out with friends and don't wander off on your own! Especially if you've just moved to the area and are unfamiliar with the surroundings. Don't leave your drink unattended under any circumstances, and if you forget and leave your drink and come back to it, I'd suggest just getting a new one.
>
> **Taylor**

While you're out and about having fun, it's really important to stay safe. Here is a list of tips to keep in mind when you're out with friends.

VANESSA'S TOP TIPS
for staying safe on a night out

> Charge your phone before you go out and make sure you have spare money to get home. Keep it in a separate compartment so you don't spend it at the bar.
>
> **Aimee**

- Tell someone about your plans.
  - Who you are going out with and where, and let them know what time you're expecting to get home.
- Avoid going out straight from university when you have your laptop and any other expensive equipment.
  - It's not worth the risk, take your things home first.
- Make plans for how to get home:
  - Keep taxi money in your bra/pocket away from your purse/wallet (and don't spend it during the night!)

- Make sure you have a local taxi number programmed into your phone, and try not to wait for your taxi alone. If you find yourself on your own, then try to get to a taxi rank.
- Get the bus/tube/metro timetable cued up on your phone internet browser.

- Find a safe walking route.
  - Some cities and universities have Safe Walking Schemes. One example is Strut Safe (which has a free phone number and app and is a service now available in multiple cities in the UK) and don't walk home alone.

- Make sure your mobile phone is charged (and has enough credit).
- Know your limits when it comes to alcohol (if you drink).
- Eat before you go out; this will help offset the effect of alcohol if you do drink.
- Never leave your drink unattended.
- Don't accept drinks or drugs from someone you don't know.
- If you think your drink has been tampered with, ditch it, and get another one.
- Try to avoid doing anything you wouldn't do sober.
  - Inappropriate touching is a common theme among those out and about, and it's not limited to younger adults. According to Drinkaware (2020) 1/3 of young women and 1/10 of young men have experienced inappropriate touching during a night out. Try to avoid touching anyone without their express permission. It can be tricky in a crowded bar or club, but if you keep your hands to yourself, you should be fine.

- Keep tabs on your friends.
  - It's really important to ensure you and your friends are safe while you're having fun. Make sure that you stay with your

friends during the night, and that you look out for them. Don't let your friends get so drunk they make questionable choices; look after each other so you have fun without the night turning sour.

- Don't go near any large bodies of water, such as rivers or lakes, don't climb anything, and don't attempt any stunts.
  - Alcohol lowers your inhibitions, so the likelihood of you or your friends taking risks increases. Make sure that you don't do anything dangerous while you're out on a fun night or things could take an ugly turn for the worse.
- Travel home with someone else and text your someone in Tip 1 to say you're heading home.
  - If you don't live with your someone in Tip 1 then text them when you're home as well.
- Never give your address to someone you just met.
- Never allow anyone to coerce you into making decisions you don't want to make.
  - If you don't consent to what someone else is asking then they should stop asking. If they don't stop asking, and put pressure on you to change your mind (to do anything, from another drink, doing drugs, or sex) then ask someone for help. There are lots of schemes in bars and clubs now (e.g. Ask Angela); look for notices in the bathrooms and talk to friends and/or bar staff if you have concerns about someone else's behaviour towards you.
- Do not go home with anyone you don't want to spend time with.
- If you do end up spending a consensual night with someone new, take precautions and stay safe at all times.
- Have fun!

This list of tips is fairly serious, but university is still a time for enjoying yourself and having fun alongside your studies. You should have fun during your student journey, but make sure that you are safe while doing so.

Negotiating Your Classes after a Night Out

> Lots and lots of water, paracetamol, coffee (or tea), and some breakfast! Even if you turn up and sit at the back feeling sorry for yourself, it's better than laying in bed at home missing important content! Grin and bear it, it'll be worth it.
>
> **Taylor**

You may be someone who is unaffected by hangovers, or don't drink alcohol, so you're limited to just being tired. But for the vast majority of students, it is important to remember that the majority of your lecturers were once students and can spot if you have a hangover. While we do understand the lure of student nights, we are usually well aware of when they are in the local bars and clubs—there is *always* a correlation between student night and a drop in attendance the following morning!

If you are well enough the next morning, get up, shower, and brush your teeth, turn up, and get engaged. Even if you only remember a little bit of what was said, you will feel better for having got up and moved around. Get your own personal hangover cure, and eat/drink it on the way to class. Remember, you will need coffee, paracetamol, and plenty of water; take small sips regularly throughout the day. Get a friend to nudge you if you fall asleep in class, and please try not to vomit.

What to Do When Something Goes Wrong

> Do not go anywhere alone especially if you're not in your home city. Pay attention to the knowledge of local friends and students, and always have a system in place for if you and your friends are separated. It seems dramatic, but it is always better to be safe than sorry.
>
> **Cassie**

This is the section to avoid if you think it might be triggering. However, if you can't read it, please make sure your friends do. Keeping each other safe at university is very important. Much of the official advice centres around social situations in public places, but it is important to remember that these situations can occur in any situation where multiple people are present.

Unfortunately, as we are all well aware, despite all the precautions taken, sometimes things can go terribly wrong during or after a social evening/event. The core elements of where to get support when something goes wrong are covered in Chapter 13, but here we will look at what to look for, and what to do, in the event that something negative happens on a night out.

Remember, the university support systems are there for you in all situations, including those which occur off-campus. This includes university counselling services, security teams, on-campus police, and all anonymous reporting methods provided.

Drink Spiking

> Do not accept drinks or substances from strangers.
>
> **Cassie**

Things to look for (Drinkaware, 2020):

- A difference in how your drink tastes.
- Feeling sick or drowsy.

What to do:

- Tell a security guard, member of the bar staff, doorperson, etc.
- Call (or ask someone to call) an ambulance if the condition of you or your friend deteriorates.

Assault—Non-Sexual

> *Do not be pressurized into doing social events you do not want to. Follow your own path.*
>
> **Abbie**

If you or one of your friends gets involved in an altercation with others, try to extricate yourselves peacefully and diplomatically, if it is safe to do so. There are all sorts of reasons why altercations might take place, but all of them need diffusing safely if possible.

However, this can be challenging, particularly in situations where alcohol is involved. If you struggle to extricate yourself or your friend from the situation, and in the event an altercation with others crosses over into physical assault, contact the doorperson or security team if you can, then call the police.

You and your friends should ensure that you drink water from this point on, and call time on your night out. There is a possibility that you may all be required to give a statement to police if the altercation is serious, and you want to be as sober as possible when this happens.

Assault—Sexual

Always ask for help.

Emma

Sexual relationships are a normal part of life, and it is important to re-member that all sexual relationships require mutual consent. Where one party does not consent then a sexual relationship should not take place. Unfortunately, sometimes interpersonal connections between two individuals can take a darker turn where one individual does not appropriately account for the important rules around consent. Sexual activity where one party does not consent (or is coerced into consent-ing) is classified as sexual assault and is against the law. If this happens to you or anyone you know, it is really important to remember that nobody is to blame for anything that happens to them without their explicit consent.

Rape Crisis UK is a useful resource (https://rapecrisis.org.uk/) if you, or a friend, experience sexual assault. If you feel that you need support to go through any of the official steps, the staff there are a really supportive team who are experts in supporting people in this position.

If you or your friend is the victim of rape and/or sexual assault, the official advice from the Metropolitan Police is to do the following:

- Call the police immediately.
  - Do not wait. It is vital that you undergo any tests quickly as DNA evidence can disappear, and date-rape drugs can be metabolized very quickly. The tests that need to take place are not pleasant but they can dramatically improve your odds of any subsequent prosecutions being successful.
- If the assault took place on the premises of a club or pub, contact the doorperson, security team, and bar staff.

- Call a third party connected to the victim (partner, sober friend, parent, sibling, or other responsible person) to come and be with them for comfort and support.

  – Make sure you have their permission, and it's best to make sure you have that before you all go out.

- Contact an external organization for advice and support.

  – The Metropolitan Police recommend: *Rape and Sexual Abuse Support Centre* on 0808 802 9999 (12–2.30 p.m. and 7–9.30 p.m. every day). There are other sources of support listed in Chapter 13, some of which are available 24/7.

Remember, it is your choice to follow the official advice, and if you choose not to that is at your discretion. You will find that there is considerable support at university in this situation. Support staff and your academic staff will all be able to offer support (see Chapters 7 and 13).

Being an 'Active Bystander'

> Don't be afraid to say no to going out with friends. If they're true friends, they'll wait.
>
> **Kathy**

We recognize that some interpersonal behaviours are incredibly negative and can be distressing for those who are exposed to them, and universities are intended to be safe spaces where students can learn without fear of prejudice or discrimination. An 'Active Bystander' is someone who supports others either directly, when it is safe to do so, or by getting/accessing help so that others can be safe from negative interpersonal behaviours.

Some universities run a programme which can teach you how to recognize the early warning signs of situations where prejudice, abusive or negative interpersonal behaviours might occur. They can also teach you when it is safe to intervene (and how to do so), plus who to ask for help, as a way of supporting your friends and fellow students. Your own university might have an internal anonymous reporting system so that you can ensure your own safety while reporting concerning behaviour from others.

Being aware and alert to warning signs that encompass all types of negative interpersonal behaviours, from prejudice-based abuse and hate crime, to sexual and interpersonal abuse, is important in staying safe while you are at university and out socializing. By learning to recognize the warning signs for abusive or negative behaviour, you can help protect your friends and those around you from potentially damaging situations.

The central web source for this initiative lies with the University of Exeter (2020—see link in the References at the end of the chapter). This contains a tool kit of resources to support students in being aware of negative interpersonal behaviours, along with reviews of the study and a list of national support services for a very wide range of negative interpersonal situations.

You may also find that your university was part of the study and runs its own version of a course around being an 'active bystander'. If so, make sure you do it. Just remember, only intervene if it is safe to do so; if it's not then let the university and/or external organizations (such as the police) know.

Getting the Appropriate Support at University

> Find someone, or some service, that you think you can trust.
>
> **Milo**

If you are impacted by the negative after-effects of issues following a night out during your degree, you will need support while you are at university, and so you need to know whom to contact. There is support available, and you should make use of it as soon as you can. In BOX 11.1 below, fill out the core contacts you will need for university. While this information is in other sections of the book, having this here at this point is important for speed and reducing any concerns if a negative event takes place. You should keep in mind that the staff at university should be completely supportive of your position and there should be no judgement about your particular personal situation.

Obviously, it is always good to be prepared, and I hope you never have to experience any of these types of events. All being well, your time at university will be full of safe nights out that end in laughter rather than tears.

BOX 11.1 Who to Contact at University in the Event of a Negative Experience Following a Social Event

Person to contact (you can contact all or one of these, they can share information with the others as appropriate)	Email	Phone Number	Availability Hours
Personal Tutor			
Programme Leader			
Trusted Lecturer if you prefer			
Support Services			
Chaplain or Religious Leader			
Campus Security			
Campus Police			

A Final Word

> Remember that life/'fun' doesn't stop just because you're a student—you will have to fit this into your schedule, because in the real world you can't just focus on your job, the 'fun' in life shouldn't stop when you're employed, and neither should it stop when you're a student.
>
> **Aisha**

It's important to have fun at university, fun absolutely doesn't stop when you're a student, but it's important to balance this with your studies and other responsibilities. Make sure you don't over-do the social side and you don't skip classes because of a night out. And remember, it's really important to stay safe and keep an eye on your friends when you're out having fun.

 www.oup.com/he/parsonle

Visit the online resources where you will find additional materials including guides on time management, financial planning and budgeting, mindfulness and mental health, hints and tips, as well as all the tables from the book.

References

Drinkaware (2020). *How to Stay Safe at University*, https://www.drinkaware.co.uk/advice/staying-safe-while-drinking/how-to-stay-safe-at-university, accessed 13/9/2020.

HESA (2022). *Data and Analysis: Where Do Students Study*, https://www.hesa.ac.uk/data-and-analysis/students/where-study/ accessed 27/10/2022.

The Metropolitan Police (2020). *What is Rape and Sexual Assault?*, https://www.met.police.uk/advice/advice-and-information/rsa/rape-and-sexual-assault/what-is-rape-and-sexual-assault/ accessed 13/9/2020.

University of Exeter (2020). *The Intervention Initiative*, http://socialsciences.exeter.ac.uk/research/interventioninitiative/ accessed 20/9/2020.

Chapter 12

SOCIAL MEDIA, SAFETY, AND DIGITAL SECURITY

Why This Chapter Is Important

- Navigating the digital world is an essential part of undergraduate studies in the 21st century, social media and technology are everywhere, and university is no exception. For those that do want to use social media, knowing how to use it as a learning resource will benefit you in your studies.

- Many lecturers and universities use social media, and many incorporate it into their support provision and teaching. Knowing how to navigate this element of university is really useful.

- Staying safe online and keeping an appropriate balance is an important consideration on social media, this chapter covers some ways in which you can do this.

- There are safeguarding and disciplinary policies in place to ensure your safety, so knowing about these is useful to ensure you stay safe while you're studying.

> Social media . . . can become a big distraction which will cost you dearly if you can't part with it for a few hours to study.
>
> *Jamie*

The vast majority of people, of all ages, engage with social media now, and it's become a core part of how we communicate with our friends and family. You will also find that all universities, and individual departments, have a strong social media presence, typically Facebook, Twitter, and Instagram, occasionally Snapchat. Often this is marketing and promotional, but social media is also used as a source of digital support. Some lecturers also use social media as part of their teaching methods: you might find social media tools being included in learning materials. Before you get to university, check out the social media for your course and all the relevant support systems (e.g. library, Student Support, your course, and the Students' Union), and follow/like them all.

Social media can be a powerful tool to help you during your studies, but it does come with some challenges that are worth pointing out and remembering. We want you to stay safe online and on social media, so while you are with us, you are protected by our various policies pertaining to this, something the vast majority of universities now have. These policies are sometimes listed in the Student Handbook (or Student Guide), or can be listed separately. You should make sure you read the Handbook (or Guide) so that you know how to stay safe online, what we expect from you, and what you can expect from us (see BOX 12.1).

BOX 12.1 Social Media Policy

My university has a Social Media policy	YES/NO
The Social Media policy is located here	
My university has a safeguarding policy	YES/NO
The safeguarding policy is located here	
My university has a complaints procedure	YES/NO
The university complaints procedure is located here	
My university has an on-campus police presence	YES/NO
The on-campus police phone number is	

Social Media as a Learning Resource

It's a good method of communication and distributing questionnaires and methods of collecting data, but sometimes it's just a distraction. Try and have a rule that while studying avoid any form of social media unless necessary.

Bethany

Universities use social media quite a bit for promotion and sometimes subject-specific course initiatives. Keeping up to date with what's going on at university is always beneficial, and if your course has any social media pages or groups, you should definitely join them. This will give you up-to-the-minute information about your course and anything that is happening that you need to know about.

The 'big 3' are still the most popular at university—Facebook, Twitter, and Instagram. Most universities have a social media profile on these three platforms so, whichever is your preference, have a look for all the societies and departments you can find connected with your university. Snapchat is increasingly popular among university communication teams, although as the content is transient by nature, it is less useful as a learning resource than the 'big 3'.

All social media is styled in a particular way for a particular purpose, and your university and department will use the best resource for the job at hand, be that Facebook Groups for discussions or Twitter/Instagram/Snapchat feeds for announcements and all of them for information sharing. Just remember that you are under no obligation to sign up or follow anyone on social media; all course-specific information will be relayed through more typical university channels (e.g. email or VLE/module announcements) so that every student has all the information they need. Plus, the key university messages (not course or programme information) will often be on a central intranet (private internet accessed only by staff and students) as well so there is a central point of information dissemination you can check.

Social media is a fairly diverse resource that can prove really beneficial to your studies so if you don't normally use it, then it's worth thinking about, just for the duration of your course and to communicate with peers. There are lots of organizations, journals, and academics on social media, and they often report on their latest studies or work on these platforms. Twitter is particularly good for finding friendly academics to follow and learning about their latest research.

Separating Work and Play

> Turn it off while doing assignments so you are not tempted to have a look.
>
> **Deborah**

Social media is fun, but it can be very distracting. While it's always a good idea to avoid it when you're trying to concentrate on your studies, it can also be a tool to help you with your studies. Finding a balance between fun, distraction, and legitimate study/work is crucial if you're going to make social media work for you while you're at university. Working out how to stop looking at social media can be challenging, and those of you who are prone to procrastination may well find you get lost in a 'scroll hole' whenever your to-do list starts building up.

You might have the self-control to just ignore social media, which is brilliant. However, if you're a bit like me, you need to do something other than just put your phone to one side. You might find just turning your phone off, or turning off notifications, works for you during the periods you need to study. But you might find that deactivating your accounts temporarily is more effective in preventing you being distracted. There are also apps you can download that will help you control the amount of time you spend on social media.

During busy periods and exam season in particular, you do need to make sure you have a strategy in place for how to minimize your use of social media. It's a good idea to make a contract with yourself, work out what you are realistically able to do, and then stick to it. In BOX 12.2 circle all the options you think you can do, and make sure you are realistic with what measures you need to put in place to prevent yourself getting distracted by social media during your studies.

BOX 12.2 Social Media 'Distraction Minimization' Options

Social Media Checklist—Circle Everything That Applies	
I can easily ignore my phone and social media, I'm not worried	I can't ignore my phone or social media, so I need to work out a plan to stop it distracting me
I can turn my phone off easily during busy periods	I can't turn my phone off as I need to be contactable (work/ children/family)
I am comfortable turning off notifications for my social media accounts	I have to have notifications on so that I can be contactable (work/ other)
I am comfortable turning off notifications temporarily for my social media accounts	I have to have notifications on all the time so that I can be contactable (work/other)
There are no real consequences to removing social media apps from my phone	There would be an external consequence if I removed social media apps from my phone
There are no real consequences deactivating my social media accounts for a short period during study	There would be external consequences if I deactivated my social media accounts for short periods

BOX 12.2 should give you an idea of what you can realistically achieve to minimize how much social media might distract you; use this to create your own contract with yourself for busy periods. There are no rules with social media use; as long as you don't spend your classes scrolling through newsfeeds, academics don't mind as long as you complete your work to the best of your ability. If social media is a distraction for you then figure out a way to manage that within the boundaries of your own life. A digital detox is always a useful exercise anyway, but time it for periods when you have lots of deadlines or during exam season. You will know what stops you looking at social media, so utilize those tactics at busy times of the year.

Social Media—How to Make it Work for You at Uni

Social media can also be a good tool to keep in contact with friends made, or in groups set up for group assignments.

Hannah

As a general rule, notifications can be problematic and create a lot of pressure to check your phone. Social media itself is great, but constantly feeling like you need to check it because your phone is pinging notifications through can be very stressful. My best piece of advice here is to *turn off the notifications*! You're not deleting anything and you can check when you have time and are in the right headspace to do so. Turning off notifications takes the pressure off and means you are in control of when you check what's going on and you're not missing out. Anything that is actually urgent at university will always be emailed to you directly, or if you're worried about being contacted by someone about anything urgent (e.g. your child's school), remember that they will ring you; they won't send you a social media message.

Using social media to create digital study groups is a great idea; you can bounce ideas off each other and work together to understand what you are being taught. I fully recommend these, and they can be a great source of support during university. WhatsApp is a great tool when you have a small group working together, although for larger group numbers you might want to use another platform (such as Microsoft Teams™ or Google Chat™) that is easier to navigate with larger groups.

One thing to remember though is to watch out for something called 'social loafing', even within social media chats and group communications via social media such as WhatsApp. This is when someone in your group effectively just watches you do all the work, then takes it for themselves so they don't have to do anything. You want to avoid this; make sure you only engage in group chats with those who you are working well with, and never, ever share your assignments, especially via social media.

It's wonderful to help out friends who are struggling for a period of time, but if someone doesn't contribute to your online study group, politely ask them to contribute or to leave. You get to control who you connect with on social media, so never let anyone pressure you into making a connection or including them.

Boundaries and the Future

> Be aware that social media reflects on your future. Imagine you are an employer reading your posts, reflect before you post.
>
> **Chantelle**

How you manage your social media use now will help set you up for your social media use in future employment. It's useful to remember that future employers will potentially look at your social media sites during the application process, so if you're sharing on your open social media accounts that you bunked off class to go to the pub, it's likely to impact their decision to ask you for interview. Make sure you keep your social media private and only post what you'd be happy to talk to others about in public. Remember, social media is like a party: just because you control the guest list does not mean you can control who is looking through the window or if there will be any unexpected guests.

Boundaries

> It can be hard but remember, they are there to help and educate, not to be your friend
>
> **Christa**

You do need to remember that your lecturers, and academics you interact with online, are not your friends. We are your educators, not your peers and that boundary needs to be maintained. Everyone has a code of conduct to follow in universities, both staff and students, that covers behaviour both face-to-face and in a virtual online capacity. So, no matter how fun your tutors might be, make sure you keep to the boundaries of what is considered appropriate behaviours, which are much like for standard communication with academic staff in person or via other electronic communications. For example, liking a picture of their cat on social media, or saying how much you enjoyed their class or latest article is completely fine, but sharing intimate details, making advances, assuming intimacy, trolling, or discussing violence in any format is obviously completely inappropriate.

WhatsApp is a popular communication tool, and while it can be tempting to use WhatsApp to communicate, please remember it is a private messaging media rather than something to be utilized particularly in your studies or used to communicate with staff. Within

WhatsApp, your personal phone number will be visible to everyone you are communicating with. As a rule, any action or request that leads to you sharing or gaining the personal contact number of a member of staff is to be avoided during your studies.

Where boundaries are crossed, there is a disciplinary process to follow where it's a member of your immediate academic community, something you will find in the social media and safeguarding policies (if one is available, see BOX 12.1) and your Student Handbook/ Guide. If you do wish to raise any concerns, my recommendation is to speak to a lecturer you trust whom you know stays within appropriate boundaries, in the first instance, and get their advice.

What to Do When Something Goes Wrong

> *Be cautious not to post anything inappropriate or hateful, as a report of inappropriate activity could lead to serious consequences.*
> **Hannah**

Social media is fun, but as with everything in the digital world, there is a darker side. Lots of things can go wrong with social media, from people you don't know getting in contact with you and communicating in a negative manner, to unwanted messages and pictures appearing on your timeline and in your messages. And of course, you need to make sure you are not the one sending unwanted messages and/or images to others.

What you don't want to be is that student that others are complaining about. Your use of social media should be respectful and mindful of others' boundaries at all times. You don't need to 'like' every post, you don't need to send dozens of messages or post lots of comments. Sometimes individuals can lack awareness that they are not the central person in another's life. Where you find yourself in a one-sided conversation, take the hint that the other person needs some space or does not wish to communicate with you at that time. This is not necessarily a reflection on you, it simply means you need to respect their wish for space.

Where individuals do cross boundaries and you don't want to communicate with them, blocking someone can help give you control over who contacts you on social media, as can reporting individuals through standard social media reporting processes if they cross boundaries that contravene social media policy. If the individuals you need to block/report are members of the university community, you should report them to your lecturers too. There are complaint processes available to you and you should find these in your Student Handbook or online (see BOX 12.3). You should be able to contact your Personal Tutor and Programme Leader regarding complaints, but if you struggle to talk to these members of staff for any reason, you should make a note of a lecturer/tutor whom you are comfortable talking to—that way you will have multiple avenues of help when you need them.

Sometimes individuals can fall under the influence of others, and this can lead to them changing their behaviours (e.g. eating less, suddenly attending a new religious group, rejecting their friendship group). It can be difficult for students to know what to do in these situations. All universities have a safeguarding team, this is a team of people from across the university who protect the welfare of their students, visitors,

BOX 12.3 Complaints Policy and Process

My university has a complaints policy	YES/NO
The complaints policy is located here	
My Personal Tutor is	
My Programme/Course Leader is	
Another Lecturer I know/trust is	

and any individuals who might be considered at risk from harm, either from others or to themselves. Safeguarding teams also aim to protect those students vulnerable to being drawn into terrorism or extremist groups, working within the Prevent UK strategy to ensure individuals are supported in getting out from under the influence of others.

If you have any concerns about the safety of yourself or others, be that online or offline, for any reason, you should contact a lecturer you trust and ensure you contact the central university teams as well, so that any issues can be resolved and you, or the relevant individuals, can be supported appropriately through existing safeguarding and support teams. We don't want our students to be unsafe, and if you or they are at risk of harm, either through being targeted or through the influence of others leading to behaviour changes, then we want to know so that we can support you, and them, effectively.

Inappropriate Behaviours: Cyberbullying, Trolling, and Revenge Porn

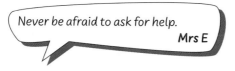

Never be afraid to ask for help.

Mrs E

What you'll find, after reading through your university Social Media Policy (and this chapter), is that you need to be quite careful about how you use social media. Remember that you should only post on social media what you'd be happy to say to someone's face, or what you are happy with others (potentially future employers) reading. Trolling and negative comments, including cyberbullying, are likely to lead to disciplinary procedures if they are reported, with the potential for police involvement in the most serious cases. So, make sure you are professional and respectful in all your posts to fellow students, services, and staff.

Table 12.1 contains some core definitions of the major categories of inappropriate behaviours that can carry a risk of prosecution.

Table 12.1 Definitions

Concept	Definition
Cyberbullying	Where one or more individual negatively target a particular individual with the intent to cause embarrassment or humiliation. This can include sending, sharing, posting, or creating negative content that might be harmful, false, personal, and private.
	Unlike physical bullying, a single act is all that's needed to qualify as cyberbullying.
	While cyberbullying itself is not illegal, individuals can be prosecuted under various other acts (e.g. the Protection from Harassment Act 1997).*
Cyberstalking	The repeated use of targeted electronic resources, such as the internet, to harass, frighten, and intimidate someone over a sustained period of time.
	Cyberstalking is difficult to prove, but it is illegal under UK law, carrying a maximum penalty of ten years in prison.*
Trolling	The act of leaving a message on the internet to upset someone. Messages are typically harmful and hurtful, but can also be obscene, indecent, or offensive.
	You can be prosecuted for trolling offences and this can lead to up to two years in prison in the UK.*
Revenge Porn	Where individuals upload intimate sexual images or videos of another person without permission, with the intent to cause harm, humiliation, or embarrassment.
	You can be prosecuted for revenge porn offences and this can lead to up to two years in prison.*

* Source: The Crown Prosecution Service, UK. https://www.cps.gov.uk/

It is important to be familiar with these so that you are able to be vigilant while on social media in particular. While most people do not experience any of these, they are on the rise and something that you should be mindful of when using social media and digital communication tools.

Privacy Online

Make sure you keep your social media private and limit who can access it. This is great advice generally, as you should always make sure you have secure passwords for all your digital devices (minimum 16 characters with some capital letters, numbers, and non-letter characters), but in the whirlwind of social activity that can sometimes happen at university, it's particularly important to keep in mind. If you don't want your profile and messages to be accessible to everyone, lock them down and restrict access. There are plenty of tools for this on all social media platforms, make the most of them. Check out the privacy settings and lock your profiles down as much, or as little, as you like. Remember, it is *your* space, you get to invite, and disinvite, whoever you choose.

Sometimes privacy settings and blocking individuals through normal social media channels is not enough, and occasionally an interaction started on social media can spill over into your life and start impacting your classes and mental health. This is where talking to a lecturer and a member of support services will help, you will be directed to contact the Police as well for the more serious cases. Within the social media policies is advice on what to do when something negative happens to you: follow this advice. If you're not sure, ask a tutor. But never leave a negative situation to get out of hand. We understand the role social media plays in everyone's lives now, so don't be afraid to ask for help. There is more on this in Chapter 13.

Keeping a Level Head When All Around Are Losing Theirs

> There'll always be someone who does better than you . . . focus on yourself.
>
> **Alice**

Social media is a wonderful tool to connect with others, but it can also be a source of stress. Fear of Missing Out (FOMO) means that we tend to put notifications on, check constantly, and connect with lots of people we don't actually know. However, all this can put us at risk of added stress, emotional imbalance, and potentially connect us with some not very nice people.

Sometimes, social media is not good for your mental health, even under normal circumstances. Sometimes nobody can agree, sometimes you think everyone is doing better than you, and sometimes it all gets a bit too much. You have to remember that social media is just a collection of tools, and that *you* are in charge of what you see on your social media.

If you don't want like what is happening in a group, leave the group. If everyone posts their grades on the day marks are released and you don't like seeing that, then avoid social media on those days. If you find yourself getting distracted when you need to concentrate on assignments or revision, try to put it to one side.

If you do find that social media is making you particularly unhappy or mentally unwell you should try to be more proactive and deactivate your accounts, or delete the apps from your phone. Social media is just a tool to connect to other people, which is great, but it shouldn't be used if it makes you stressed or unhappy, so make sure you only connect with those people you know and/or like.

A Final Word

> *No private messaging on social media, that's what email is there for. Remember this is a professional relationship and whilst they will support you with any issues outside of university that may affect education inside, they are there as a professional tutor not a friend.*
> **Kaylie**

Social media is a wonderful tool for connecting with others, but it's easy to end up getting distracted by it and it can be far too easy to compare ourselves to others. There are also dark corners of social media that are best avoided if possible. Be selective with how you use it and turn notifications off, or avoid it completely, when you need to get work done. While it's fine as a resource and tool, it's a big distraction that can potentially negatively impact on your work. If you do use it, then make sure you follow the social media channels provided by your unviersity and department; used properly, social media can be very beneficial in supporting your studies. And remember, if you do need help when something goes wrong, just ask for help.

www.oup.com/he/parson1e

Visit the online resources where you will find additional materials including guides on time management, financial planning and budgeting, mindfulness and mental health, hints and tips, as well as all the tables from the book.

Chapter 13

ACCESSING SUPPORT

AN OVERVIEW OF SUPPORT WHEN YOU NEED IT MOST

Why This Chapter Is Important

- Your time at university is a significant and sustained period in your life, so it stands to reason that there will be challenges to overcome at some point, most of which you won't be able to predict. This chapter goes through the support resources available and what to do when you face challenges in your life which can impact on you and your studies.

- There is a wide variety of support available at all universities, covering all aspects of personal and academic matters. While you are at university you have access to completely free, confidential support for all the challenges you will face during your time with us. This chapter shows you what support is available and gives you space to write down the all-important details just in case you ever need them.

> Don't get disheartened, the journey will be full of ups and downs, and as clichéd as it sounds, you take the rough with the smooth.
>
> **Dylan**

Hopefully, everything will go smoothly for you when you're at university, but it is always good to be prepared for the challenges that life can sometimes throw at us all. This chapter will focus closely on where you should turn if you need support when something goes wrong during your studies, be that in your personal life or your academic life. There is a little bit of repetition here from previous chapters, with a few expanded tables and boxes provided, but this saves you from flicking back through the book when you're stressed and worried. If you are someone who worries about losing information, complete the tables here, take photos and email them to yourself; that way you will have the information in several places if you need it.

Life doesn't stop while you're studying for your degree, and two to four (or more) years is a long time. We all go through natural life events during long periods of time, and this is something that staff at universities are fully aware happens with our students as well. Don't worry, we plan for this within universities, with all services and faculty members working together to ensure students are supported in their studies. There is a whole range of policies and procedures to support you, should you come up against events where you need some extra support for a while.

Of course, if in doubt, always contact your Personal Tutor, who will be able to answer all the questions you have and direct you to the most suitable forms of support available. The sooner you let staff know there are things you're dealing with the better. We can help with most things if we know early enough, so if you're struggling with anything, either inside university or externally, let us know and ask for support from your lecturers and the support teams we have in place for you.

Academic Help and Support

> Seek help, as daunting as it can be, it will be the best thing you can do for yourself. There are people ready and waiting to help you. I struggle with a mental health illness and the support I received has helped my confidence and self-esteem, this has helped me be a more engaged and confident student.
>
> **Mariam**

Studying at university is a challenge, particularly if you've been out of education for a while. Sometimes you might need some basic help with your work, such as interpreting feedback and/or improving your work. Or you could have a more basic question like getting hold of necessary software or technical access to the VLE (virtual learning environment). I'll go through each major source of support in turn, and there are boxes to complete in each sub-section. In all instances, you can go to your Personal Tutor, the Module Leader, your Programme Leader, and any other lecturer on your programme that you trust (see BOX 13.1). I have added an additional space for a lecturer you know and/or trust. While there are people you are directed towards in a formal capacity, there are often many lecturers you talk to regularly while at university. In particular, with sensitive issues, it is important that you talk to someone you trust. We would rather you talked to someone other than the 'official person' than not talk to anyone at all; your trusted contact will recommend you speak to the relevant people, but we can always privately share necessary information (with your permission) if you prefer.

BOX 13.1 Key Contacts on Your Course

Person	Name (and Module Details)	How to Contact Them (e.g. Email/Microsoft Teams/Phone)	Where They Can Be Found (Office and Office Hours)
Programme Leader/Director (or Course Manager/Leader)			
Personal Tutor			
Module Leader			
Module Leader			
Module Leader			
Module Leader			
Module Leader			
Module Leader			
Another Lecturer I trust			

The Library and Study Skills

> *If I'm struggling with something, they can explain it.*
>
> **Kallie**

Your library is likely to have a huge set of resources to deal with most academic issues. These resources are available on campus, online, and support sessions are now typically delivered both in a face-to-face and online capacity so that all students can access them. There will be staff on hand, both in person within the libraries, and/or via online chat mechanisms who can help you with finding information about borrowing books (and any fines you might incur), finding journal articles, or general queries.

You might also find there is a raft of study skills resources available through the library website that you can access. Study skills support is sometimes available within the library, and sometimes by specialist teams; however, support for study skills will likely always be advertised within the library, so they are a good first port of call if you need academic help. Within the support available you might find that there are Study Skills sessions available to help with academic writing and related aspects of your studies. You can go to these sessions for support in developing your writing skills, so if you struggle with writing you should make use of these resources.

Complete BOX 13.2 by going to your university website and putting in the relevant information. Remember those leaflets and induction tours you went on in Freshers' Week? There's probably some information there too, so have a look at those if you still have them. There is an extended version of BOX 13.2 in the Online Resources for this book. So if your university has a lot of information on this, make a note here that you've completed the bigger table in the Online Resources.

BOX 13.2 Resources Offered by The Library

Resource	When Available	Where Available
Librarian		
Study/Academic Skills Support		
Academic Writing Sessions		

Technical Issues

> It is important to get help and ask the university for additional support
>
> Kyle

In a world of continued technological advancement there is increasing reliance on the use of computers and gadgets to complete daily tasks, and universities are no exception. You may have a fully online course, be doing a hybrid/blended learning course, or be fully on campus for your classes. Whichever format your course takes, we rely on technology to make it all work and deliver all your materials to you (through your VLE), so you will need to know how to access everything, and if something goes wrong with the digital side of your studies, you will need to let someone know fast or you will fall behind. Fortunately, there is always technical support available. In BOX 13.3 fill in the sections to make sure you know where to go in a technical emergency.

BOX 13.3 Technical Support Services

Resource	When Available	Where Available
Technical Help Desk		
Online Support (IT Support Portal)		
Technical Support Contact (in your Department)		
Library-based Technical Staff (if available)		
Other technical support option (if available)		

What Can Academic Staff Do?

> It does change a lot when the lecturers believe in you
>
> **Alice**

Academic staff can help you with most of the issues that touch on, or are affected by, academic matters while you're at university; they can also help you get support for anything that happens during your degree that impacts you. But you do need to remember that no matter how supportive they are, they are not counsellors. Most academic staff will be happy to listen but we can't always directly help; we will always refer you to any additional support services you need to access, so you should make sure you take advantage of these.

Assignment Deadlines and Extensions

> If one of your children becomes ill and you have a deadline looming, speak to your lecturer they can and will support you, so do not struggle in silence.
>
> **Emma**

It's important to remember that assignment deadlines are not negotiable. Get organized and plan in advance when you get your deadlines for each module. However, we are aware that sometimes unexpected events happen (such as illness) that prevent you completing or submitting your work, and we have policies in place to deal with this. We are more than happy to give you extra time if you need it, although hopefully this won't happen; just remember to ask and don't assume you will have this extra time.

All universities have some regulation around how long extensions can be. The crucial piece of advice here is to make sure you contact the Module Leader as soon as possible (preferably before the deadline) and explain why you need the extension. We have policies to follow and some situations aren't covered. Be clear and up front with us in your initial email; remember, what you tell us remains confidential.

For all extensions to deadlines, you would usually contact the Module Leader first (or the person who is running the module and dealing with extensions, this can vary between universities). This is not necessarily the tutor who teaches your class, so look to see who is listed as being in charge of the module on the VLE. Contact the Module Leader directly as they will be the one who deals with extensions on their modules.

Extenuating Circumstances (Mitigation)

> *Take time out from assignments/independent study when you begin to feel overwhelmed. It'll benefit you so much more.*
>
> **Aimee**

Sometimes an extension isn't enough, and you need to simply do your assignment at another point in time. It might be the case that life events impact one or more assignments and you feel like you're falling behind in your work due to serious situations beyond your control that significantly impact your ability to complete assignments; for example, hospitalization for yourself or family, or a death in the family. You will always get one more chance to do the assignments during your studies (this is automatic at every university), but you want to be able to get your actual marks rather than a capped mark. We allow all students to attempt assignments again if they fail a module, but if they've had one attempt, or didn't have a reason not to submit, the mark is usually capped at the basic pass mark (typically 40%). Applying for extenuating circumstances (sometimes called Mitigation) gives you a chance to explain why you were unable to complete the work on time and request that your next attempt is not capped at the pass mark.

When you consider applying for extenuating circumstances, it is important to remember that you are delaying your assignments, and you will have to do the work at a later date during that academic year; the assignments don't go away. Make sure you consider what you can, and can't, manage to do carefully. Discussing your situation with your Personal Tutor and/or Programme Leader is really important; they may have recommendations that you will want to follow that are in your best interests on the course. For example, they may recommend a mixture of extensions and extenuating circumstances, depending on your particular situation, or they may recommend a leave of absence (something we cover in the next section). The crucial thing is to communicate and talk to us. We can only help if we know there is a problem. In BOX 13.4 you can put all the information you'll need if you have to apply for extenuating circumstances.

BOX 13.4 Extenuating Circumstances (Mitigation) Procedures

Resource or Service Details	Contact/Source Information (Website/Email/Phone Number)
What my university calls Extenuating Circumstances/Mitigation	
Where I can find the policy	
Where I can find the application form	
Where to send the form	
Who to send the form to	
Who to talk to on my course if I apply for Mitigation/ Extenuating Circumstances	
Personal Tutor	
Another Lecturer I trust	

During your time at university we don't just look after you when you're on campus. It is important to remember that we are aware that life itself can impact your studies, and that life happens off campus as well as on campus. If you are struggling with your home/work life impacting your classes make sure you contact your Personal Tutor or another lecturer you trust. You might also want to contact Study Skills and Support Services as well, depending on the situation you find yourself in.

Sometimes there is a sustained series of events that happen, which mean you fall behind in your studies and you need considerable support. If you feel like you're falling behind you should contact your Personal Tutor and/or Programme Leader. They will be able to discuss your options on the course and are best placed to help you navigate your way through extensions and extenuating circumstances, and at this point they will usually discuss a leave of absence with you if they feel it is appropriate.

Leave of Absence/Suspension of Studies

> When I felt like I was falling apart, seeing [in an email from a lecturer] 'You can do it, let's have a break, you can do it though, we'll be there when you do' … that was so important for me, that literally changed everything in that moment
>
> **Sarah**

Sometimes life can really get in the way of academic study, so you may need a break from university while you sort things out. There are many reasons this might be the case: financial problems, illness, maternity leave, personal issues, or mental health challenges.

All universities offer the option for students to take a leave of absence (sometimes called a suspension of studies), which can be a short period or a whole academic year, depending on what is possible for your course. This is something you can look up online, but you will need to go and see your Programme Leader if you want to take this option and my advice is to do this first. They can talk to you about what it means for your studies and what you will need to do before (and when) you get back. Talking to someone at the start of this process is vital in making sure you feel supported in this step of your studies, and ensures you get the most accurate advice for your course.

There can be financial implications for taking a leave of absence so you will need to discuss the situation with the finance team at your university as well, something you will be directed towards as part of the process. More details about finance can be found in Chapter 2, but it is important to remember that you will usually only get funding for active years of study. If you pause your studies your student finance will be recalculated, and your funding will also pause. If you have taken a leave of absence part-way through a term, it might be that you have been overpaid and the student finance team will require repayments of part of your loan.

In BOX 13.1 you'll find a space where you can put the names and contact details for all your core course contacts so that you can access them if you need them.

Withdrawal

Sometimes a leave of absence (or suspension of studies) can lead to a student withdrawing from the course completely, or it might be that you are unable to continue your studies at this time and need longer than you have access to through the leave of absence procedures. In this instance it is important to get advice and support while you have access to the resources within university.

Make sure you discuss all your options with your Programme Leader and/or Personal Tutor, look at whether reapplying for a place on your course in the future is an option, and what steps you might take to access external sources of support once you leave university. You will also have to update the finance team about your plans as your university finance will be stopped and recalculated at the point of withdrawal, and again, this can lead to potential repayment depending on the point you've reached in your studies. See Chapter 2 for more information about loans and repayments.

It is important to note that while payment schemes can be put in place for any repayments you need to make, you will need to repay any overpayments from the current academic year in a fairly short time frame, and not at a later date like with completed years of student finance.

Who to Talk to When Something Goes Wrong

> Don't be afraid to ask for help. I struggle with PTSD, chronic anxiety, and depression but I have never felt so supported in my life. Don't shy away from problems.
>
> **Aisha**

All the people on your course who teach you can support you through all academic matters, from tutors in class to your Personal Tutor, Module Leaders, and Programme Leaders. We work in conjunction with the support services to ensure you get the support you need, that is well-being-based rather than academic, when you need it. This is why your academic tutors are often a good first port of call when things go wrong. We can rapidly put in place a lot of things that will support you while you need a little extra help during your studies, while simultaneously directing you to the information and support services you need to access.

We have a set of procedures in place for when things go wrong, and we try to direct students who need help to the quickest source of support. There are often particular people you need to go to who will have dedicated time to support students. If you experience any problems relating to your course, or situations/personal experiences that are impacting your course, use Table 13.1 to work out who to contact.

Table 13.1 Who to go to when things go wrong

Issue	Person to Contact	Service to Contact
Missed assignment deadline	Module Leader	None
Forgot about an assignment completely	Module Leader	None
Extraordinary factors that prevent you doing work right now (e.g. breaking your arm, illness)	Personal Tutor Programme Leader	Support/Well-being Services
Work conflicts with unsympathetic employer	Programme Leader	None
Home conflicts that are impacting doing work	Personal Tutor	Support/Well-being
Pregnancy	Programme Leader	Support/Well-being (if needed)
Minor illness	Module Leader	None
Severe illness	Module Leader Programme Leader	None
Disability-related issues	Programme Leader	Disability Support/ Enabling Team
Mental-health decline	Personal Tutor	Well-being/Support Services

(Continued)

Table 13.1 Continued

Issue	Person to Contact	Service to Contact
Suicidal ideation and serious concerns about mental health	Personal Tutor	Support/Well-being Services Crisis Team (NHS Service) Counselling Services
Bereavement	Personal Tutor	Support/Well-being Services Counselling Services
Visa problems	Programme Leader	International Office
Having to suddenly go home (local, national, or international) for family reasons	Programme Leader Personal Tutor	None
Assault (on or off campus)	Personal Tutor	Campus Police (if on campus) Safety Team Local Police (if off campus) Counselling Services
Discrimination (any form)	Personal Tutor	Campus Police Safety Team Support Services Well-being Services
Drug- and Alcohol-related concerns	Personal Tutor	Mental Health Services National Helplines
Child/Parent/Family Concerns and issues	Personal Tutor	Support Services
The impact of changes in interpersonal differences and situations	Personal Tutor	Support Services Counselling Services
Financial difficulties	Personal Tutor Programme Leader	Finance Support
All other issues	Personal Tutor	As needed

Where I've listed Personal Tutor, you can also contact an additional lecturer you know and/or trust if that is easier for you. There is also, as mentioned in Chapter 7, a whole raft of support services available for you throughout the academic year. Again, which one to contact in individual situations is listed below.

As with any list, this one is not exhaustive; I can't list all the different situations that might mean you need some extra support, but I've listed the most common ones we see. For all others, please contact your Personal Tutor, or another lecturer you can trust, in the first instance, they will be able to direct you to the most appropriate sources of support.

Financial Support

> [There is] a great support system, and it can be for an array of issues, it's not just a counsellor, [there are] people to talk to about childcare, money, and so much more, you know that you'll be well looked after.
> **Hannah**

In Chapter 2 we covered finances while at university. Sometimes students' financial situations become precarious, through sudden changes in employment, unexpected significant costs, loss of finances, or any other serious financial situation that can directly impact the student and put their studies at risk. For these situations you can apply to something called a Hardship Fund or an Emergency Fund. Most universities have something in place for this situation.

These funds are only available through application, and if you're not sure, go and see the Finance Team at your university, In BOX 13.5, you'll find some headings relating to this: fill these in, and make sure that if you begin to struggle financially you let the finance team know. You should also let your Personal Tutor know.

BOX 13.5 Financial Hardship Support

Person/Service	Contact Details/Location of Information
Finance Support Team	
Hardship Fund	
Personal Tutor	
Another Lecturer I know/trust	
Students' Union	

The Students' Union is another resource that can provide support during difficulties, including financial. They have emergency financial support options available to you, so they are another source of support. You will find details of what is available on your university's Student Union website. As with the hardship funds, you will likely have to apply to access financial support.

Wrap-Around Care at University

You are overwhelmed with support and services to help you on your path. You only need to ask or look on the website and you'll find a variety of support services.

Charlie

We know that while you're at university there are many things in your lives which can impact both you and your studies. While you are studying at your university, it is very important to remember that you can access the support services for anything that happens both on, and off campus; we don't forget about you once you leave class, we look after you throughout your studies. If something happens while socializing (see Chapter 11), or if something has happened at home (see Chapters 8 and 9), this can still impact you, and your studies. We recognize this and you can use the support available within university to help you through any issues you experience outside of your academic studies.

In BOX 13.6 make sure you complete the contact details and opening hours for all services listed. If the name isn't quite right for your university,

BOX 13.6 University Support Systems

Service	Email	Phone Number	Opening Hours	Drop-In Sessions
Mental Health Support Team/Support Services				
Counselling Support				
Welfare Support/Adviser				
Disability Support/Enabling Team				
Finance Support				
Study Skills/Academic Skills Support				
Students' Union				
Equality and Diversity Support				
Chaplaincy (covers all religious faiths and communities)				
Other University Religious Contacts				
Security Services/Safety Team				
Campus Police				

just amend it in the 'Service' column underneath what I've written; that way you won't be wondering what someone is referring to if they ask you to seek support from a particular university service. You might find the same service at your university covers many different aspects of what is listed in this table below; for example 'Well-being' is a good term that is sometimes used as a central hub for many different services.

Outside Term Time

> *There is plenty of support for students from all backgrounds/ religions.*
>
> **Jamie**

It's important to remember that support services run throughout the vacation periods. There may be reduced staffing due to staff needing to take annual leave, but there will always be cover in place. If you need to access support services or library support during vacation periods, don't hesitate to do so.

Contrary to popular belief shared by the media, your lecturers do not have all the vacation periods off on holiday, we work through most of them. During your vacation periods, academic staff are still busy preparing and marking work, doing research, or getting on with personal work projects. There will be short periods when we're not available while having some annual leave, and we will set an 'out of office' email when this is the case. But it is usually the case that there will be academic support available through most vacation periods, so if you need to contact a member of staff, make sure you email us; if you receive an automated reply in response, check what we've written on it and when we'll be back checking emails again. If there is a delay and you need urgent support, contact the support teams.

There is one exception to this: closure days. There are some days when universities do close down completely, generally for a short period over Christmas and Easter. During these periods, you can still email staff, but you will usually need to wait for a reply until the next working day after the university opens up again. If your support needs are urgent, you should call an external source of support, and we'll cover that in this next section.

External Sources of Support

> The biggest tip would be to talk to someone! It's scary starting somewhere, and if you let someone know of any pre-existing disorders [they] can put something in place to make your time at university easier.
>
> **Cameron**

As mentioned in Chapter 7, there are many sources of support available for you in the UK, for all the myriad support needs you might have. While we provide a huge range of support for you at university throughout the year, we can't be available 24/7 most of the time, so outside of normal university hours you will need other sources of support until we open again in the morning, or open up again after closure days.

There are some nationally recognized sources of support for students: Student Minds and Nightline being two of the most well known. There will be a local Nightline in your area, and you should find the local contact details and add them to Table 13.2.

Table 13.2 External Sources of Support

Organization	Website	Contact Number
SAMARITANS	www.samaritans.org.uk	116 123 (24 hour)
STUDENT MINDS	www.studentminds.org.uk	Ring Samaritans (see above)
MIND (mental health support)	www.mind.org.uk	0300 123 3393
REFUGE—domestic violence support	www.refuge.org.uk	0800 2000 247 (24 hour)
PAPYRUS—Suicide Prevention Charity	www.papyrus-uk.org	0800 068 4141
ALCOHOLICS ANONYMOUS	www.alcoholics-anonymous.org.uk	0800 917 7650 (24 hour)
NARCOTICS ANONYMOUS	www.ukna.org	0300 999 1212
NATIONAL GAMBLING HELPLINE	www.begambleaware.org	0808 8020 133
RAPE CRISIS	www.rapecrisis.org.uk	0808 802 9999 (to find local services)
VICTIM SUPPORT	www.victimsupport.org	0808 168 9111 (24 hour)
BEAT—eating disorder support service	www.b-eat.co.uk	0808 801 0677 (adults) 0808 801 0711 (for under 18s)
FAMILY LIVES—parenting support (including bullying)	www.familylives.org.uk	0808 800 2222
RELATE—relationship support	www.relate.co.uk	Find your nearest Relate contact number through the website
SWITCHBOARD (LGBT+ support)	chris@switchboard.lgbt	0300 330 0630

(*Continued*)

Table 13.2 Continued

Organization	Website	Contact Number
THE MIX (support for under 25s)	www.themix.org.uk	0800 808 4994
SANEline (mental health support)	www.sane.org.uk	0300 304 7000
NIGHTLINE	www.nightline.ac.uk	My local number is:
STONEWALL	www.stonewall.org.uk/	0800 050 2020
MERMAIDS	https://mermaidsuk.org.uk/	0808 801 0400
INTERSEX EUROPE	https://oiieurope.org/	Not a support helpline like the others, but a great resource. See website for more details.

All support services listed below are anonymous unless you wish to disclose information, so you can be assured that nothing will be shared without your permission. Check individual privacy notices if you have any concerns at all. This is by no means an exhaustive list, and the NHS has a long list of support service details available for a whole range of additional situations.

Sometimes you might need to access local healthcare if you are unwell, so BOX 13.7 gives you a space to write down the contact numbers in your local area. If you have moved away to university but are relying on your home doctor or dentist, it is always good to register at the local NHS practices closer to your university and/or where you live during term time. If you are ill, you won't necessarily be able to travel, so register at your local practices so you can get healthcare when you need it.

BOX 13.7 Local Healthcare Services You Can Access

Service	Contact Number/Location
My local GP Surgery (Doctors)	
My local Dentist	
My local NHS Walk-in Centre	
My nearest A&E	

A Final Word

> Believe in yourself and continue to work hard, you're there because you deserve it, and anything is possible when you tell yourself 'I can' instead of 'I can't'.
>
> **Jessica**

There is a plethora of resources available to support students while they study at university and you should never feel embarrassed or anxious about accessing this support. Hopefully you will sail through university without any problems. But if you do have any worries or concerns, or anything unexpected happens in any area of your life that you need some support with, don't worry, help is available. Having read through this chapter and hopefully completed the various boxes you will be in a better position to seek help as and when you need it. There are lots of sources of support for you while you are a student with us, so make sure you use them. The most important thing you should remember from this chapter, is to talk to us, and let us help you get the support you need.

www.oup.com/he/parson1e

Visit the online resources where you will find additional materials including guides on time management, financial planning and budgeting, mindfulness and mental health, hints and tips, as well as all the tables from the book.

Index

Notes: Tables and boxes are indicated by an italic *t* or *b* following the page number. *vs.* indicates a comparison.